HANDBOOK OF INFORM........

ON

THE PORT OF MILWAUKEE

Issued By

K. A. ALBRECHT
HARBOR TRAFFIC DIRECTOR
Under Authority of The
BOARD OF HARBOR COMMISSIONERS
MILWAUKEE, WISCONSIN

TABLE OF CONTENTS

Page

FOREWORD

All large cities are located where there is a break between land and water transportation. While other elements influence their growth, the size of a city is more completely controlled by its transportation importance than by any other factor.

Because of our limited railroad facilities, the citizens of Milwaukee have, from its earliest history, always been harbor-minded. They have ever recognized the savings effected and loyally supported lake shipping improvement. This explains in part the general popular support of the movement to develop the best Municipally Owned Harbor on the Great Lakes. In pursuance thereof, Milwaukee has acquired all but a few hundred feet of its lake water front. Part of this area is being filled in and developed for drive, recreational and park purposes, the balance set aside for harbor needs. This land when completely revetted and filled in will comprise 231 acres with a frontage of two and one-half miles on Lake Michigan.

Milwaukee's greatest economical opportunity appears to lie in two directions: namely, as a recreational and as an industrial center. Its central location and temperate climate with other factors have long made it a popular convention center. This asset, together with the importance of tourist traffic into Wisconsin, make the wisdom of beautification of our water front and environs more than of local value.

As an industrial city our growth has been phenomenal. We claim the greatest diversity of industry of any community. The high grade mechanics who early came to us with their industrious and thrifty habits have not only been a leading contributing factor in this achievement, but help to explain why we have the least crime, the largest home ownership and the best governed large city in the United States.

In conclusion, it may be said that with the Great Lakes conveying more tons of cargo than the Atlantic Ocean between the United States and Europe; with the growth of tonnage on the lakes far exceeding that on the ocean; with the unparalleled advance of industry and population in the district southwest of Lake Michigan; with the high type of citizenry here about, Milwaukee has judged rightly in preserving and promoting municipally, its great asset, the harbor; and is destined to become a much greater factor as a leading industrial center of the world

MAYOR D. W. HOAN.

MILWAUKEE HARBOR, WISCONSIN

Location and description—Milwaukee harbor is on the west shore of Lake Michigan, distant about 85 miles northerly from Chicago and about 83 miles west of Grand Haven, Michigan. It is located at the mouth of the Milwaukee River and consists of a channel protected by piers and of an outer basin, having an area of about 1,200 acres, in which vessels seeking safety from storms, and those awaiting berth, can be moored; the basin is protected by a breakwater about three miles long, extending from the north shore at McKinley Beach, in a generally southerly direction, connecting the shore again at Russell Avenue. The present commercial harbor is in the Milwaukee, Menomonee and Kinnickinnic Rivers.

AIDS TO NAVIGATION

MILWAUKEE BREAKWATER LIGHT STATION: Located at Southeasterly end of North Breakwater, on North side of the main entrance through the Breakwater to outer harbor. Station is of most modern type, stands in 33 feet of water, and under water portion is concrete caisson, with concrete superstructure pier above water, 54 ft. by 60 ft. by 20 ft. high. The pier is surmounted by a two-story steel building. The roof of the building is surmounted by steel tower, two stories high, housing the Diaphone fog signal instrument in top story, and the lantern house stands on top of the tower. Building and tower are painted red. Focal plane of lantern at 67 feet above water, light visible sixteen miles. Lantern is equipped with fourth order "fixed" lens, illuminated by electric light controlled by "Sign Flasher," showing characteristic of red flash every six seconds (10 flashes per minute), light 4.5 seconds, eclipse 1.5 seconds, candlepower 5,000.

Fog Signal is an air Diaphone, characteristic, group of two blasts every twenty seconds, first blast 1 second, silent 2 seconds; second blast, 1 second, silent 16 seconds. A radio mast supporting the far end of antenna stands 73½ feet high in the breakwater 200 feet Northwest of station. The radiobeacon transmits continental code, letter "M", two dashes, during foggy weather. Every 180 seconds groups of two dashes for 60 seconds, silent 120 seconds. Radiobeacon also transmits daily in clear weather from 1:30 to 2:00 and from 7:30 to 8:00 A. M., and 1:30 to 2:00 and from 7:30 to 8:00 P. M. (90th meridian Central Standard Time.) Telephone Broadway 2152.

MILWAUKEE BREAKWATER ENTRANCE SOUTH SIDE LIGHT: A white pyramidal skeleton steel tower located on South side of main entrance on concrete base, on the North end of South breakwater. Focal plane at 47 feet above water, visible 10 miles. Lens illuminated by acetylene gas compressed in acetone. Characteristic, white flash every two seconds, white light 1 second, eclipse 1 second, 190 candlepower. The flashing of light is controlled by automatic flasher, and the light is cut off during day time by sun valve.

MILWAUKEE NORTH PIERHEAD LIGHT: Cylindrical tower, painted red, standing on outer end of North Pier. Focal plane 45 feet above water, visible 14 miles. Light is furnished from a fourth order fixed lens, illuminated by electric light, showing a fixed red light of 1,700 candlepower. every ten seconds. Light and fog signal are operated by Keepers through the cable by remote control from Breakwater light. Telephone Broadway 2301.

MILWAUKEE SOUTH PIERHEAD LIGHT: Located at the outer end of South Pierhead is a pyramidal shaft painted white. Focal plane of lens is 41 feet above water, visible 8 miles, candlepower 70. Characteristic of light flashing white every 3 seconds, flash 0.3 seconds duration (20 flashes per minute.) Lens is illuminated by acetylene gas and flash is produced by automatic flasher, and under control of sun valve.

MILWAUKEE BREAKWATER SOUTH ENTRANCE LIGHT: A structure very similar to the South Side light will be established about 1929 on completion of the Breakwater construction by the U. S. Engineers, on the Northerly side of the South Entrance gap through Breakwater. The tower will be 34 ft. skeleton steel on a concrete base, with focal plane at 47 feet above water, and will then show a flashing red light illuminated by compressed acetylene.

MILWAUKEE NORTH POINT LIGHT: Located in Lake Park on high bank at North Point at Northerly limit of Milwaukee Bay. Octagonal Iron tower, painted buff, 74 feet high, standing on 80 foot high bank of Lake. Focal plane above water 154 feet. Characteristic, fixed white light 1,800 candlepower, visible 18 miles, with white flash of 1.6 second duration, every 30 seconds, 9,100 candlepower, visible 22 miles. Lens is a fourth order revolving, with flash panels. Telephone Lakeside 5129-J.

MILWAUKEE LIGHT SHIP

One of the familiar sights in Milwaukee's harbor is the lightship "MILWAUKEE," maintained by the U. S. Lighthouse Service in addition to the various fixed aids to navigation.

The "MILWAUKEE" is located in 50 feet of water, 3 miles due east of the harbor entrance pier heads, and approximately 2⅖ miles east of the breakwater. The ship is of steel construction, painted red, with the name in large white letters on the side of the ship. It has a length of 108 feet, beam of 23 feet, and carries a crew of nine men.

The light is mounted above a circular gallery on her mast, at an elevation of 45 feet above water. It is of 1,900 candlepower, and is visible for 14 miles. The light flashes in groups of 15 seconds, consisting of 3 flashes of 1 second each, followed by a long flash of 8 seconds, each flash intermitted with an eclipse of 1 second.

The ship's fog signal is a 12-inch steam chime whistle, which signals with 2 unequal blasts every 60 seconds. The first is of 3 seconds duration, silent 7 seconds; the second, 4 seconds duration, silent 46 seconds.

LS

A red steel spar buoy, marked M, is located about 0.1 mile west of the "MILWAUKEE" as a guide to her position.

The boat is relieved for docking and overhauling every two years.

WEATHER FORECASTS AND STORM WARNINGS
U. S. Weather Bureau, Federal Building
METEOROLOGIST—Wm. P. Stewart.
(Telephone Broadway 8600)

The United States Weather Bureau, a division of the Department of Agriculture, plays an important part in Milwaukee's Marine life through its broadcasting of storm warnings and forecasting of weather conditions.

The Weather Bureau issues a daily bulletin forecasting weather conditions for Milwaukee and vicinity, for Wisconsin and for Lake Michigan. The ordinary weather predictions are also broadcasted over the three radio stations at stated times.

When approaching severe weather conditions are indicated, the prediction is telephoned to the three local radio stations and the announcements are made immediately.

Small craft, storm and hurricane warnings are displayed by means of pennants by day and lanterns by night from the staff of the sewerage disposal plant adjacent to the harbor entrance, so that ships leaving the port are fully warned as to what to anticipate in the way of weather conditions. The various storm warnings are indicated as follows:

THE SMALL CRAFT WARNING.—A red pennant indicates that moderately strong winds that will intrefere with the safe operation of small craft are expected. No night display of small craft warnings is made.

THE NORTHEAST STORM WARNING.—A red pennant above a square red flag with black center displayed by day, or two red lanterns, one above the other, displayed by night, indicates the approach of a storm of marked violence with winds beginning from the northeast.

THE SOUTHEAST STORM WARNING.—A red pennant below a square red flag with black center displayed by day, or one red lantern displayed by night, indicates the approach of a storm of marked violence with winds beginning from the southeast.

THE SOUTHWEST STORM WARNING.—A white pennant below a square red flag with black center displayed by day, or a white lantern below a red lantern displayed by night, indicates the approach of a storm of marked violence with winds beginning from the southwest.

THE NORTHWEST STORM WARNING.—A white pennant above a square red flag with black center displayed by day, or a white lantern above a red lantern displayed by night, indicates the approach of a storm of marked violence with winds beginning from the northwest.

HURRICANE, OR WHOLE GALE WARNING.—Two square flags, red with black centers, one above the other, displayed by day, or two red lanterns, with a white lantern between, displayed by night, indicate the approach of a tropical hurricane, or of one of the extremely severe and dangerous storms which occasionally occur.

Storm warnings are displayed in this manner during the period of navigation, approximately from the 10th of April to December 15th.

7

REGULATIONS TO GOVERN THE SPEED OF VESSELS ENTERING OR LEAVING VARIOUS HARBORS ON LAKE MICHIGAN

THE LAW

See Sec. 4 of river and harbor act of August 18, 1894, as amended August 8, 1917, published in U. S. Laws on pages 33-37.

THE REGULATIONS

West Shore—In conformity with the above law the following rule and regulation is prescribed (July 19, 1904):

The speed of all vessels and other water craft entering or leaving the harbors of Menominee, Michigan and Wisconsin; Algoma, Kewaunee, Two Rivers, Manitowoc, Sheboygan, Port Washington, MILWAUKEE, Racine and Kenosha, Wisconsin, and Waukegan, Illinois, shall be reduced to and shall not exceed a rate of four (4) miles per hour.

REGULATIONS TO GOVERN THE OPENING OF DRAW BRIDGES WITHIN THE LIMITS OF THE CITY OF MILWAUKEE, WISCONSIN, PRESCRIBED BY THE SECRETARY OF WAR, FEBRUARY 27, 1911.

See Sec. 5 of the river and harbor act of August 18, 1894, published in U. S. Laws on pages 33-37.

In pursuance of the foregoing law, the following regulations for opening the drawbridges operated by the city of Milwaukee, Wisconsin, the Chicago & North Western Railway Company, and the Chicago, Milwaukee St. Paul & Pacific Railway Company, across the Milwaukee, Menomonee and Kinnickinnic Rivers within the limits of the city of Milwaukee, are prescribed:

THE REGULATIONS

For all bridges owned or operated by the city of Milwaukee across the Milwaukee, Menomonee, and Kinnickinnic Rivers, except bridges across the Milwaukee River north of and including Buffalo Street bridge.

Section 1. The draws of the above-named bridges shall be immediately opened for the passage of foreign vessels and "vessels of the United States" as defined by section 4311 of the Revised Statutes, at all times during the day or night except between the hours of 6:15 a. m. and 7:00 a. m. upon signals to be given by blasts of a horn or steam whistle as follows viz: For the West Water Street bridge across the Menominee River and the Kinnickinnic Avenue bridge across the Kinnickinnic River, four short blasts; for all other bridges specified in this section, three short blasts Provded, That the exceptions as to hours stated in this section shall not apply to vessels having a license to carry 50 or more passengers when proceeding to or from their regular landing places on their regular trips, nor to vessels carrying United States mails, nor to fire boats of the city of Milwaukee, nor to vessels belonging to the United States.

Section 2. In case street traffic shall have been delayed by reason of the draws of any of the above-described bridges having been continuously open for five minutes or more for the passage of any of the vessels before described, the draws of said bridge may be closed, but shall be again opened for the passage of said vessels as soon as practicable: Provided

That in such case the opening of any of the above-described bridges for the passage of any vessels before described shall not be delayed more than five minutes after the proper signal is given.

Section 3. The draws shall, when the above-described signals are given, be opened as soon as practicable for all other vessels which can not pass the closed bridges: Provided, however, That no vessel of this class shall be delayed for a longer period than fifteen minutes.

Section 4. In case the draws can not be immediately opened when the signals are given, a red flag or ball by day or a red light at night shall be conspicuously displayed.

For all bridges owned and operated by the city of Milwaukee across the Milwaukee River north of and including the Buffalo Street bridge.

Section 1. The draws of the above-named bridges shall be immediately opened for the passage of foreign vessels and "vessels of the United States" as defined by section 4311 of the Revised Statutes, at all times during the day or night except between the hours of 6:15 a. m. and 7:00 a. m. and 12 noon and 1 p. m., upon signals to be given by blasts of a horn or steam whistle as follows, viz: For the Point Street bridge across Green Bay Canal, two short blasts; for all other bridges specified in this section, three short blasts: Provided, That the exception as to hours stated in this section shall not apply to vessels having a license to carry 50 or more pasengers when proceeding to or from their regular landing places on their regular trips, nor to vessels carrying United States mails, nor to fire boats of the city of Milwaukee, nor to vessels belonging to the United States.

Sections 2, 3, and 4 are same as sections similarly numbered, above.

For all bridges owned and operated by the Chicago & Northwestern Railway Company, and the Chicago, Milwaukee, St. Paul & Pacific Railway Company, across the Milwaukee, Menomonee, and Kinnickinnic Rivers within the limits of the city of Milwaukee.

Section 1. The draws of the above-named bridges shall be immediately opened for the passage of foreign vessels and "vessels of the United States" as defined by section 4311 of the Revised Statutes, at all times during the day or night, upon signals to be given by blasts of a horn or steam whistle, as follows, viz: For the Chicago, Milwaukee, St. Paul & Pacific Railway bridge across the Menomonee River at W. Water Street, and the Chicago & North Western Railway bridge across the Kinnickinnic River between Kinnickinnic Avenue and Clinton Street, four short blasts; for all other of above-described bridges, three short blasts; except when a passenger or mail train is actually ready to pass over the bridge; but in no case shall the opening of any of the above-described bridges for the vessels above described be delayed more than seven minutes after the signal is given.

Sections 2 and 3 are same as sections 3 and 4, respectively, above.

ORDINANCES OF THE CITY OF MILWAUKEE

CHAPTER XVI
HARBORS, RIVERS AND BRIDGES
ARTICLE I
OPENING AND CLOSING OF BRIDGES
SIGNALLING APPARATUS ON BRIDGES AND ABUTMENTS

Section 688. The commissioner of public works is hereby required to provide, construct and arrange in the best and most practicable manner at each of the several bascule and swing draw bridges over the Milwaukee, Menomonee and Kinnickinnic rivers and all other navigable waters of the city of Milwaukee the following signalling apparatus:

On every swing draw bridge a red light on each end of the draw piers, a red light placed as low as practicable on each free end of each protection pier, and a red light on each side of the pivot pier. The red lights on the sides of the pivot piers shall be placed where the pier is crossed by the axis of the bridge and below the floor level of the same. There shall also be placed on each of said swing draw bridges three square lanterns on the top of the draw span, which shall be raised fifteen feet above the top of the draw, and each shall show green along the axis of the draw and red at right angles to the axis. The said lanterns shall be so placed that when the draw is shut there will be shown up and down stream three high red lights above the permanent low lights; when open, green lights will be seen in line up and down the stream with the permanent red lights showing the width of the openings.

On every bascule bridge a red light on each end of the roller piers placed as low as practicable, and on each lift near the point where they touch and on the up stream and down stream sides a square lantern suspended free to swing behind a frame containing a circular panel of red and green colored glass, the frame to be attached to the end of each lift. Said last mentioned lights shall be so constructed, placed and arranged that when the bridge is closed there will be shown on the up stream and down stream sides two red lights close together in the center of the bridge and above the permanent low red lights; when completely open, two green lights will be seen at an elevation on each side of the opening and above the red lights, the latter showing the width of the opening. All of the lights hereinbefore mentioned shall be permanent.

On each abutment of all of the several bascule bridges a red ball and bell, and on each swing draw bridge, at or near the center thereof, a red ball and a bell. Each such ball shall be attached to a staff in such manner that the ball may be raised and lowered; such staff to be erected in the case of bascule bridges on the bridge houses thereof, and in the case of swing draw bridges on the superstructure thereof. Such ball shall be of such size and so placed that when elevated it can be readily seen from the river both above and below the bridge. Each such bell shall be of such size and so placed as to be heard a distance of six hundred feet both above and below the bridge.

RINGING OF BELLS UPON SIGNAL FROM VESSEL

Section 689. Whenever any vessel approaching any of said bridges shall give the signal for the opening thereof, and such vessel shall be within six hundred feet from such bridge, the bridge tenders on each side of such bridge, if it be a bascule bridge, or the bridge tender in the center thereof, if it be a swing draw bridge, shall ring the bell or bells thereon. In case any such vessel when giving the signal for the opening of such bridge shall be more than six hundred feet from such bridge, the bridge tender on each side of such bridge, if it be a bascule bridge, or the bridge tender on the center thereof, if it be a swing draw bridge, shall ring the bell or bells thereon before such vessel reaches a point six hundred feet from such bridge. In case the bridge tender on any bridge shall know that for any reason such bridge cannot be opened, he shall not ring the bell thereon.

SIGNAL PREPARATORY TO OPENING

Section 690. The ringing of the bell at the center of any swing draw bridge, or the ringing of the bells on both abutments of any bascule bridge in answer to the signal from any vessel for the opening thereof shall be a signal to such vessel that the bridge tenders thereon are at their proper posts of duty and have heard the signal on such vessel, but shall not be construed to be a signal that such bridge will be opened for the passage of such vessel.

OPENING OF BRIDGE UPON SIGNAL

Section 691. Whenever any vessel shall have signalled for the opening of any such bridge, and the bridge tenders thereon shall have rung the bells thereon as provided in section 689, the bridge tender or bridge tenders shall start to open such bridge before the distance between such vessel and such bridge shall have become shorter than the distance within which such vessel can be stopped, provided that such bridge tender or tenders shall not start to open such bridge until the same shall have been cleared of all persons using such bridge as a highway.

SIGNAL FOR OPEN AND CLOSED BRIDGE AT DAY TIME

Section 692. Whenever any such bridge shall be opened in the day time for the passage of any vessel, the bridge tender or bridge tenders thereon shall lower the signal ball or balls thereon immediately after such bridge shall start to open. Before starting to close such bridge the bridge tender or tenders thereon shall raise such ball or balls. Such balls shall be raised at all times except as above provided in this section.

SIGNAL TO PROCEED AT DAY TIME

Section 693. The lowering of such ball shall be the signal to such vessel that such bridge will be opened and that such vessel may proceed toward such bridge; but no act on the part of any bridge tender or any other person in the day time other than the lowering of such ball or balls shall be construed to be an invitation to any vessel to proceed to and through such bridge or as an indication that such bridge will be opened.

SIGNAL TO PROCEED AT NIGHT

Section 694. Whenever any vessel shall approach any swing draw bridge in the night time, the appearance of the three green lights in a line up and down stream above the draw of such bridge shall be a signal to proceed to and through such bridge.

Whenever any vessel shall approach any bascule bridge in the night time, the appearance of the green lights at the top on each side of the openings and above the low red lights shall be the signal to proceed to and through said bridge.

No act upon the part of any bridge tender or any other person in the night time, other than the appearance of said green lights as provided in this section, shall be construed as an invitation to any vessel to proceed to and through such bridge, or as an indication that such bridge will be opened.

12

LIMIT OF APPROACH FOR VESSELS BEFORE SIGNAL TO PROCEED

Section 695. It shall be unlawful for the owner or owners, officer or officers, or other person or persons in charge of any vessel or vessels navigating the navigable waters of the city of Milwaukee to approach any nearer to any of the bridges over the said rivers than to a point at a distance from such bridge within which such vessel can be stopped without colliding with such bridge while said signal balls are up or elevated in the day time, or while said green lights are not displayed in the night time.

PENALTY

Section 696. Every bridge tender or other person in charge of any such bridge who shall fail or neglect to promptly raise or lower such bridge signal ball as provided in section 689 hereof, or who shall knowingly or intentionally fail or neglect to open any such bridge as provided in section 691 thereof, shall upon conviction thereof be punished by a fine of not less than five dollars nor more than ten dollars, or by imprisonment in the house of correction of Milwaukee county for not to exceed thirty days.

CLOSING OF BRIDGES AGAINST VESSELS

Section 697. Bridge tenders or persons in charge of bridges shall not close the same against vessels seeking to pass through until passengers, teams or vehicles have been delayed five minutes by the bridge being open.

ALTERNATION OF PASSAGE THROUGH AND OVER BRIDGES; HOURS DURING WHICH CLOSED

Section 698. Whenever, between the hours of six o'clock in the morning and eight o'clock in the evening, persons, teams or vehicles have been delayed at said bridges five minutes by reason of said bridges being open for vessels to pass; it shall be the duty of the bridge tenders or other persons in charge of the bridge or bridges, to raise the signal ball and immediately close the same and keep the same closed for fully five minutes for such persons, teams or vehicles to pass over, if so much time shall be required, when the same shall be opened again and be kept open (if necessary for vessels to pass) for the like period; provided, however, that bridge tenders shall not open or swing any city swing; draw or bascule bridge across the Milwaukee, Menomonee or Kinnickinnic rivers between six fifteen and seven o'clock a. m., and in addition to the morning hour shall not open or swing any city swing, draw or bascule bridge across the Milwaukee river north of and including Buffalo street bridge between twelve o'clock noon and one o'clock p. m.; and provided, further, that the exceptions as to hours stated in this section shall not apply to vessels having a license to carry fifty or more passengers when proceeding to or from their regular landing places on their regular trips, nor to vessels carrying United States mails, nor to fire boats of the city of Milwaukee, nor to vessels belonging to the United States.

PENALTY

Section 699. Any person or persons who shall violate any of the provisions of section 695 shall be chargeable with whatever damage may result to the city by reason of any such violation, and shall also be subject to a penalty of one hundred dollars for each and every such violation; and in case the same person or persons shall violate such provisions, or any of them, a second or more times, the court before which the trial is had may, in addition to the penalty or fine authorized as aforesaid, also imprison such offender or offenders not exceeding three months.

COMMISSIONER OF PUBLIC WORKS
TO ENFORCE

Section 700. It shall also be the duty of the commissioner of publ works, so far as in his power, to see that the provisions of this artic are fairly and faithfully observed; and when necessary he shall call upo the chief of police for aid to enable him to do so.

ORDER OF VEHICLES WHEN BRIDGE IS OPEN

Section 701. All drivers of single or double teams attached to an wagon, hack or other vehicle who may congregate with their teams in th immediate vicinity of any swing, draw or bascule bridge erected over river or any navagable waters in the city of Milwaukee, during the time an such bridge is in process of being opened, or about being opened, shall tak their places in regular order as they drive up near such bridge, and avoi all crowding or attempt to get ahead or in advance of any other vehicle nor shall any driver enter, or attempt to enter with his wagon, hack o other vehicle upon any bridge during the time of its being opened, no until such bridge is placed back in safe position.

POLICE TO PRESERVE ORDER; PENALTY

Section 702. Any member of the police department is hereby en powered to give any direction for the preservation of good order and th equal convenience of the public, on or near any bridge in the city of Mi waukee; and any person refusing or neglecting to obey such order, or wh shall violate either of the provisions of section 701 shall be subject to ar rest, and, upon conviction, shall pay a fine of not less than five dollars, no more than fifty dollars, with the costs of prosecution, or may be imprisone in the house of correction of Milwaukee county for not more than sixt days, in the discretion of the court.

BELLS TO BE RUNG BEFORE OPENING

Section 703. It shall be the duty of the several bridge tenders of th city before opening the bridges, or either of them for any purpose what soever, to ring the bell or bells thereon.

RINGING OF BELL A WARNING SIGNAL

Section 704. The ringing of the bell or bells on any of the bridges re ferred to in section 688 shall be a warning and signal to all persons ap proaching such bridge on the highways leading thereto that said bridg is about to be opened, or is open, and that it is dangerous to proceed towar said bridge.

DRIVING ON DRAW AFTER SIGNAL IS GIVEN PROHIBITED

Section 705. Any person or persons who shall walk or attempt to walk or who shall drive or attempt to drive on the draw of the aforesaid bridge with a team of any description, either double or single, or who shall ride o attempt to ride on the draw on the aforesaid bridges with a horse or othe animal, or propel any automobile, bicycle or other similar vehicle on th draw of the aforesaid bridges, after the tender of such bridge has com menced to give the signal for swinging or opening the bridge, shall b deemed guilty of an offense, and shall be liable to a fine of not more tha five dollars, nor less than one dollar for each and every such offense, or t imprisonment in the house of correction of Milwaukee county for not mor than thirty days, in the discretion of the court.

LOITERING ON BRIDGES

Section 706. Any person or persons who shall stand or sit or loiter o any of the aforesaid bridges or the abutments or railing appertaining t the same, provided that the bridge is in passable condition, shall be deemed guilty of an offense and shall be liable to a fine of not more than five dollars nor less than one dollar for each and every violation of this section, or to imprisonment in the house of correction of Milwaukee County for not more than thirty days, in the discretion of the court.

MEDDLING WITH BELLS

Section 707. Any person or persons who shall ring or meddle with the bell or bells on any bridge, except the several bridge tenders, shall be deemed guilty of an offense, and shall be liable to a fine of not more than ten dollars nor less than one dollar, for each and every violation of this section, or by imprisonment in the house of correction of Milwaukee county for not more than thirty days, in the discretion of the court.

BRIDGE TENDERS TO REPORT DEFECTIVE PLACES

Section 708. The bridge tenders shall immediately report all defective and dangerous places, upon their respective bridges, and the approaches thereto, which shall come to their notice, and in the performance of their duties they shall particularly examine such bridges and the approaches thereto, and make such report as aforesaid. Such report shall be made to the superintendent of bridges and public buildings, who shall forthwith transmit said report to the office of the commissioner of public works.

DUTY OF SUPERINTENDENT OF BRIDGES

Section 709. It shall be the duty of the superintendent of bridges and public buildings, under the direction of the commissioner of public works, to repair and keep in repair all bridges belonging to said city, and to do and perform such other and further work as may be deemed necessary by the commissioner of public works, and to employ such men in the prosecution of said work, under the direction of the commissioner of public works, as may be necessary.

ARTICLE 2.
REGULATIONS COVERING VESSELS IN HARBORS AND RIVERS.
INNER AND OUTER HARBORS DEFINED

Section 710. For the purposes of this article the navigable waters of Milwaukee are divided into the "inner harbor" and "outer harbor." The inner harbor shall include the Milwaukee river from Lake Michigan to the dam across said river and all those portions of the Kinnickinnic river and Menomonee river. and the canals. water channels, and slips laid out and established by authority of the city charter and amendments thereto. The outer harbor shall include all waters of Lake Michigan outside the government piers and within the government breakwater, known as the harbor of refuge. The rules and regulations contained in this article apply only to the inner harbor unless otherwise specified.

RULES FOR VESSELS LYING IN THE HARBOR

Section 711. (a) No vessel, craft, or float shall be left in the harbor without having on board or being in charge of some competent person to control, manage, and secure the same, without first obtaining permission from the harbor master.

(b) Every vessel, craft or float shall have kept on board, during the night time, a light in a conspicuous place; and all fires which may be kept on board of such vessel, craft or float shall at dark be extinguished, or so guarded, as to insure safety from fire.

(c) No vessel, craft or float shall be suffered to lie in the harbor adrift or insecurely fastened.

15

(d)   No vessel, craft, or float shall obstruct the channel or be moored or anchored so as to prevent the passage of any other vessel, craft or float; nor shall it be so moored or anchored as to range against, injure, interfere with, or hinder the opening or closing of any bridge.

(e)   No vessel, craft or float, while moored or anchored, shall work its engines, provided that the master or other person in charge of a vessel, craft, or float may work its engines for the purpose of testing them, if he shall keep some person so stationed that he can observe approaching vessels, and at the same time signal the engineer to stop the engine.   Such person shall signal to keep the engine at rest, and it shall be kept at rest while any approaching vessel, craft or float is within a distance of two hundred feet.

(f)   No vessel, craft or float shall be fastened to the protection piers of bridges, bridge approaches, or piles driven for the protection of bridge piers or approaches.

(g)   It shall also be unlawful to fasten any craft or vessel of any description to protection piers of bridges, bridge approaches or piles driven for the protection of bridge piers or approaches in the city of Milwaukee.

RULES FOR VESSELS MOVING IN THE HARBOR

Section 712.   (a)   No vessel, craft or float shall exceed the speed limit of four miles an hour; but this provision shall not apply to the tugs of the fire department while responding to an alarm.

(b)   No vessel, craft or float propelled by steam shall pass stern first through the draw of any bridge, unless towed by a tug.

(c)   No sailing vessel shall pass through the draw of any bridge, except in tow of a steam craft.

(d)   No vessel, craft or float shall be towed with its anchor or anchors down or dragging on the bottom of the harbor.

(e)   All vessels, craft or floats passing through the draw of any bridge shall do so as rapidly as is consistent with the proper movement in the river, and with the terms of this article; but in no case shall any vessel, craft or float cause any bridge to remain open for more than five minutes.

(f)   No vessel having a length of over three hundred feet keel shall do any winding at the forks of the Menomonee and Milwaukee rivers under its own steam, but shall use tugs for that purpose.

SELLING MERCHANDISE FROM VESSELS AT FOOT OF STREETS

Section 713.   It shall be unlawful for any person or persons to sell, or expose for sale, or deliver, from any ship or vessel, landed at the foot of any street or alley, in the city of Milwaukee, any wood, lumber, coal, staves or any other goods, wares, or merchandise, or to tie up or moor any vessel, craft or float at the foot of any street or alley in the city of Milwaukee; except that stone, wood, lumber, and other materials and articles, which are or may be delivered for the city of Milwaukee, or any ward thereof, and bought by the city of Milwaukee, for the use of said city, or department or ward thereof, may be so delivered if agreed upon at the time of the making of the contract therefor.

USE OF CITY WHARVES AND DOCKS

Section 714.   The harbor master of the city of Milwaukee is hereby authorized and directed to give such orders and directions as he shall deem proper and necessary to prevent the use of any wharves and docks which are owned by the city of Milwaukee, except public wharves and docks at the foot of public streets, by any boat, vessel or other craft belonging to any person, firm or corporation, excepting the use thereof by

MOTORSHIP "MILWAUKEE"

Transatlantic Service—Hamburg American Line

Courtesy Milwaukee Journal

any person, firm or corporation to whom a lease of such wharves or docks may be granted by the proper city authorities. The harbor master may order the removal at any time from said wharves and docks of any boat, vessel or other craft.

PENALTY

Section 715. Any master or owner or other person or any officer, manager or agent of any corporation, having in charge or in his control any boat, vessel or other craft, excepting the person, firm or corporation expressly excepted in the foregoing section, who shall neglect or refuse to comply, within one hour after being ordered, with any order of the harbor master authorized by the foregoing section, shall for each offense, on conviction thereof, be liable for a penalty of not less than twenty-five dollars nor more than one hundred dollars, or in default of payment thereof not less than five nor more than thirty days' imprisonment in the house of correction for Milwaukee county; and each and every day of twenty-four hours for which such neglect or refusal shall continue shall be deemed a separate offense.

ARRIVING VESSELS TO REMAIN IN OUTER HARBOR

Section 716. During the season of navigation, and when the inner harbor is crowded so that the channels are in danger of being obstructed, arriving vessels shall remain in the outer harbor until their docks are ready to receive them.

NORTH MENOMONEE CANAL

Section 717. No vessel, craft, or float shall be laid up in any part of the North Menominee canal during the season of navigation; and no vessel, craft, or float consigned to a dock in said canal shall go west of the ship yard at the so-called Sixth street bridge until her dock is ready to receive her, and as soon as unloaded, if it be during the season of navigation, she shall immediately move out of the said canal.

DUTIES OF DOCK FOREMEN, ETC.

Section 718. Dock foremen must swing their hoists out of the way promptly whenever vessels leave their docks, or when not in use; and all persons in charge of any vessel, craft or float shall cause all fenders and all other things projecting over the side of such vessel, craft or float to be pulled up and kept out of the way when not actually in use.

BLOWING OF WHISTLES

Section 719. All vessels, crafts or floats, while navigating, lying or being within that part of Milwaukee Bay which is within the limits of the city of Milwaukee, or, while navigating, lying, or being within any of the rivers or navigable waters within the limits of said city are prohibited from blowing any steam whistle for any purpose whatever, except when it shall be necessary for them to pass through any bridge within the limits of said city.

The following bridges require:

4 short blasts of the whistle—each not to exceed 2 seconds in length.

1. Bridge across the Menomonee river at the foot of West Water Street.
2. Railroad bridge, one-half block east of the above mentioned bridge.
3. Chicago & Northwestern Railroad bridge across the Kinnickinnic river, between Kinnickinnic Avenue and Clinton Street.
4. Kinnickinnic Avenue bridge.

2 short blasts of the whistle—each not to exceed 2 seconds in length.

Cherry Street bridge.

3 short blasts of the whistle—each not to exceed 2 seconds in length.
All other bridges.

PENALTY

Section 720. The owner or other person in charge of any vessel, craft or float, or any other person violating any of the provisions of the foregoing sections of this article, unless otherwise provided, shall upon conviction thereof be fined not less than ten dollars or more than one hundred dollars for each offense; and the obstruction of any channel in violation of the terms of this article for each period of twenty-four hours or part thereof shall be considered a separate offense. Every vessel, craft or float, whose owner, master or other person in charge shall become liable as herein provided, shall also be chargeable with the payment of said penalty, and the same shall be and constitute a lien upon such vessel, craft or float, to be enforced as provided by law.

INJURY TO BRIDGES, ETC.

Section 721. Whenever any person having charge of any vessel, craft or float shall wish to move the same through the draw of any bridge, reasonable time shall be allowed for the opening of the same; and any person who shall move any vessel, craft or float against any bridge, or the center or protection piers thereof, before the same shall be opened, to the injury thereof, and any person who shall otherwise, through willfulness or negligence, run any vessel, craft or float into any of the piers, cribs or docks of the harbor at the straight-cut, or into any bridge or abutment thereof, or allow such vessel, craft or float to be driven or run into such piers, cribs, docks, bridge or abutment, or who shall take any stones from the crib for ballast or any other purpose, shall be subject to a penalty of five hundred dollars for each offense, and shall in addition be liable for all damages thus caused. Any vessel, craft or float, whose owner, master or other person in charge shall become liable as aforesaid, shall also be chargeable with the payment of the said penalty and the said damages, and said amounts shall be and constitute a lien on said vessel, craft or float, to be enforced as provided by law.

DUTIES OF THE HARBOR MASTER

Section 722. It shall be the duty of the harbor master to carry into effect the provisions of this article, and, in general, to give such orders and directions relative to the location, change of place or station, manner of moving in or using the harbor, of all vessels, craft or float lying, moving or laid up in the harbor, whether in use or not in use, as may be necessary to promote good order in the harbor and the safety and convenience of all vessels, craft and floats therein, or to expedite the conduct of business dependent thereon and especially at all times to keep the channels free and clear for the passage of the tugs of the fire department.

POWERS OF THE HARBOR MASTER

Section 723. The harbor master shall have power to move any vessel, craft or float while moored in the harbor, whether receiving or discharging cargo or otherwise, when he deems it necessary to do so to facilitate the movement of other vessels, craft or float.

He shall also have power to stop at any time or place such vessels, craft or floats as may be proceeding up or down the harbor, so as to prevent a jam or blockade; and to fasten, raise or move any vessel, craft or float insecurely fastened, adrift or sunken.

19

HARBOR MASTER; HOW TO PROCEED

Section 724. Whenever it shall be necessary to move, fasten or raise any vessel, craft, or float in order to carry out the provisions of the preceding section, the harbor master shall notify the owner, master or other person who may be in charge thereof to move, fasten or raise such vessel craft or float without delay.

If the harbor master shall be unable to find the master, owner, or person in charge of such vessel, craft or float, or any person answering such description, after a reasonable search, he shall not be required to give said notice, but shall forthwith move, fasten or raise such vessel, craft or float.

EXPENSES, TO WHOM CHARGED

Section 725. All costs and expenses of moving, fastening or raising any vessel, craft or float as aforesaid shall be a lien upon the said vessel craft or float, and the proper city officers are authorized and empowered to enforce the payment of such lien in the manner provided by law.

The owner or owners of any vessel, craft or float shall also be personally liable for all such costs and expenses to be recovered by the city in suit as in personal action.

AUTHORITY OF HARBOR MASTER OVER OUTER HARBOR

Section 726. So far as it does not conflict with the authority exercised by the government of the United States, the harbor master shall have the same jurisdiction and authority and the same power in or over the outer harbor and all vessels, craft or floats moored or navigating therein as are herein given him in or over the inner harbor and the vessels, craft or floats moored and navigating therein.

POWER TO COMPEL ASSISTANCE

Section 727. The harbor master is hereby authorized and empowered to call to his aid any tug, boat or crew, or other vessels and men, to assist him in the removal of vessels, or the performance of any of his duties, and he is authorized and empowered to take any tug, vessel, craft or float that may be necessary for this purpose, and compel the assistance of any crew that he may deem necessary to carry into effect his orders.

RULES AND REGULATIONS

Section 728. The harbor master shall have power to make such further rules and regulations as he may deem necessary to carry into effect the provisions of this article and to properly perform the duties thereby devolved upon him.

POWER TO MAKE ARRESTS

Section 729. The harbor master shall have power to make arrests and to call to his aid the police department for the purpose of enforcing his orders.

PENALTY

Section 730. Any person who shall resist the harbor master, or any person acting for him, in the execution of his duties hereunder, and any person who shall fail, neglect or refuse to comply with the lawful orders of the harbor master, shall, upon conviction thereof, be subject to a fine of not less than ten dollars nor more than one hundred dollars, or by imprisonment in the house of correction of Milwaukee county for not to exceed ninety days.

ARTICLE 3.
MISCELLANEOUS
PROHIBITING DEPOSITS OF EARTH, ETC., IN RIVERS AND HARBOR

Section 731. It shall be unlawful for any person, firm or corporation, in person or by his or its agent, employe or servant, to conduct, place, cast, throw, deposit or cause to be conducted, thrown or deposited in or upon any of the waters or ice surfaces on Lake Michigan, or any river, canal or public water within the jurisdiction of the city of Milwaukee any kind of earth, sand, filth, manure, dirt, rubbish, ashes, sewerage, garbage, waste article or trade waste, or refuse or offal of any kind whether liquid or solid; provided, that this section shall not apply to substances or articles deposited or conducted into the city sewerage through lawful drains in accordance with the ordinances of the city of Milwaukee. Any person, firm or corporation who shall violate this section shall on conviction of such violation be fined not less than five dollars nor more than two hundred dollars, and in default of payment thereof shall be imprisoned in the house of correction of Milwaukee county for not less than ten days nor more than ninety days. Such person, firm or corporation shall be deemed guilty of a separate and distinct offense for every day during which such violation shall continue.

PILING LOOSE MATERIAL AT WATER'S EDGE

Section 732. No person or persons and no corporation, agent, servant or employe of any person or corporation shall place, pile, throw or maintain, or suffer, allow or permit to be placed, piled, thrown or maintained any crushed stone, coal, gravel, sand, ashes, dirt or other loose material within three feet of the water's edge of any navigable waters within the city of Milwaukee.

LUMBER PROJECTING OVER DOCK LINE

Section 733. No person or persons and no corporation, agent, servant or employe of any person or corporation shall place, pile or maintain or suffer, allow or permit to be placed, piled or maintained, any lumber or other material in such manner as to project over the dock line of any navigable waters within the city of Milwaukee.

PENALTY

Section 734. Any person or persons or any corporation, agent, servant or employe of any person or corporation who shall violate any of the provisions of the two foregoing sections shall upon conviction thereof be fined by a fine of not less than ten nor more than fifty dollars for each offense, together with the costs of the action, and on failure to pay such fine shall be imprisoned in the house of correction of Milwaukee county for not less than ten nor more than thirty days.

BUILDING ENCROACHING UPON THE WATERS OF MILWAUKEE RIVER ABOVE THE DAM

Section 735. It shall be unlawful for any person, firm or corporation, in person or by his or its agent, employe or servant, to place any obstruction, or to erect or cause to be erected any building or permanent structure of any kind encroaching upon the waters, banks or shores of the Milwaukee river above the dam. Any person, firm or corporation who shall violate this section shall on conviction of such violation be fined not less than five nor more than fifty dollars with the costs of prosecution, or shall be imprisoned in the house of correction of Milwaukee county for not less than fifteen nor more than ninety days for each and every offense.

21

SPEED OF AND LIGHTS ON BOATS ON UPPER MILWAUKEE RIVER

Section 736. No boat, launch or other craft propelled by steam, gasoline, petroleum, electricity or other motive power shall pass up or down the Milwaukee river above the dam, and within the limits of the city of Milwaukee, at a greater rate of speed than six miles an hour.

Each such boat, launch or power craft shall have and display at all times between the hours of sunset and sunrise red and green signal lights, fitted with inboard screens so as to prevent them from being seen across the bow, and of such a character as to be visible on a dark night with a clear atmosphere at a distance of at least one mile, and so constructed as to show uniformly a permanent light over an arc of the horizon of ten points of the compass, and so fixed as to throw the light from right ahead to two points abaft the beam on either side. The minimum size of glass globe shall not be less than six inches in diameter and five inches in the clear.

RENTING BOATS TO CHILDREN; LIFE-SAVING DEVICES

Section 737. No craft, either hand or power, shall be rented to children under eighteen years òf age unless accompanied by a parent, guardian or some other person twenty-one years of age.

Each power propelled boat shall be equipped with as many life-saving devices as the passenger capacity.

Each craft propelled by hand power shall be equipped with at least one life-saving device capable of bearing up the weight of any person for twelve hours.

All power propelled boats shall be required to follow a course in the center of the stream, or as near the center as possible, except when making a landing.

No power boat shall be operated with the mufflers open.

PENALTY

Section 738. Any captain, owner, mate or other person in charge or control of any boat, launch or other craft described in the two foregoing sections who shall violate the provisions of such sections shall be guilty of a misdemeanor and shall be punished for each offense by a fine of not less than ten dollars nor more than fifty dollars, or by imprisonment in the house of correction of Milwaukee County for a period not to exceed sixty days.

BASCULE, SWING AND RAILROAD BRIDGES ACROSS THE MILWAUKEE, MENOMONEE AND KINNICKINNIC RIVERS

No.	Location and Name	Kind	Miles above mouth of river	Draw Openings clear width			Clear height above low water datum
				Right	Left	Center	
	Milwaukee River			Feet	Feet	Feet	Feet
1.	Chicago & Northwestern Ry. (Jefferson Street)	Railway	0.34	87.7	87.5	...	6.2
2.	Broadway	Highway	.53	...	...	130	13.7
3.	East Water Street	Highway	.67	...	...	130	12.2
4.	Buffalo Street	Highway	.88	...	...	130	7.8
5.	Clybourn Street	Highway	1.04	...	...	77.5	11.8
6.	Michigan Street	Highway	1.13	...	...	80.4	9.3
7.	Wisconsin Avenue	Highway	1.23	...	...	70	10.7
8.	Wells Street	Highway	1.35	...	...	77	6.4
9.	Cedar-Biddle Street Bridge	Highway	1.46	...	...	100	12
10.	State Street	Highway	1.56	...	...	90.1	13.7
11.	Juneau Avenue	Highway	1.74	68	63	...	9.9
12.	Cherry Street	Highway	1.97	55	55	...	9.8
13.	Point Street (across canal)	Highway	2.02	...	...	50.4	10
14.	Walnut Street	Highway	2.24	58.2	58.3	...	8
15.	Holton Street (viaduct)	Highway	2.52	...	...	79.2	63.6
16.	Racine Street	Highway	2.9	...	...	...	22.9
	Menomonee River and Canals						
17.	Chicago, Milwaukee, St. P. & P. Ry. (West Water Street)	Railway	.02	...	75	...	7.6
18.	West Water Street	Highway	.05	...	...	80.1	8
19.	Sixth Street	Highway	.35	...	...	77.5	29.4
20.	First Avenue	Highway	.55	...	...	85	29.4
21.	Muskego Avenue	Highway	.93	...	...	70	8.0
22.	Chicago, Milwaukee, St. P. & P. Ry. (Florida Street)	Railway	.76	65.5	...	...	7
23.	Sixth Avenue	Highway	1.0	45	46	...	6.8
24.	Sixteenth Street	Highway	1.12	...	...	120	33.4
	Kinnickinnic River						
25.	Chicago & Northwestern Ry. (Foot Lapham Street)	Railway	1.0	61.8	61.6	...	...
26.	Kinnickinnic Avenue	Highway	1.45	...	...	100	9.2
27.	Chicago, Milwaukee, St. P. & P. Ry. (Ziemer Street)	Railway	1.49	...	93	...	14.4
28.	Chicago & Northwestern Ry. (Between Kinnickinnic Ave. and Clinton St.)	Railway	1.52	...	93	...	14.4
29.	Clinton Street	Highway	1.61	62	62	...	8.7
30.	Becher Street	Highway	1.84	54	54	...	10
31.	Lincoln Avenue	Highway	2.12	54	40	...	9.1

NUMBER OF BRIDGE OPENINGS
(Exclusive of Railroad Bridges)

	1926	1927
Milwaukee River	43,543	40,742
Kinnickinnic River	6,562	7,263
Menomonee River	8,994	9,832
TOTAL	59,099	57,837

WATERBORNE COMMERCE

Milwaukee's lake traffic is reaching extremely satisfactory proportions, especially during the past few years. The total tonnage for the year 1927 was the third highest in the history of the Port. The years 1913, 1914 and 1915 are the only years in which lake traffic exceeded the eight million ton mark, and the years 1913 and 1914 are the only years which have ever exceeded the 1927 totals.

The gradual increase in waterborne commerce is due to a number of factors, among them being better relationship between the railroads and steamship lines serving Milwaukee, the general trend toward water transportation due to low transportation rates, well established steamship routes on the lakes, and the natural increase in commerce due to increasing agricultural and industrial productivity.

In 1926 Milwaukee ranked twelfth among the Great Lakes Ports according to total tons of waterborne commerce. The rank varies from year to year, depending primarily on the movement of bulk commodities on the Great Lakes. During the past eight years, the rank has been as high as eighth and as low as fourteenth.

Milwaukee has ranked third for many years, according to value of receipts and shipments among the Great Lakes Ports, and because of its increasing package freight commerce, threatens to assume the leadership.

TOTAL WATERBORNE COMMERCE
As reported by U. S. Engineer's Office

YEAR	SHORT TONS	VALUE
1918	7,086,550	$362,564,868
1919	7,008,200	320,079,300
1920	5,760,569	216,381.900
1921	6.431,147	201,660,800
1922	5,602,935	281,415,200
1923	7,705,041	415.936,200
1924	6,476,414	349,913,900
1925	6,907,811	450,001,200
1926	7,537,516	411,139,900
1927	8,233,198	466,726,000

TRANSPORTATION

Adequate and diversified transportation is an invaluable asset to a city. Milwaukee is particularly fortunate in having excellent all-rail service to an extensive territory with rail rates on a parity with Chicago and lower than Duluth. The electric railroads maintain passenger and merchandise express service to points south, west and north of Milwaukee. The carferries operating all year round across Lake Michigan provide trunk line service to and from eastern territory, and are of great importance to local industries, since they represent the main factors in keeping Milwaukee on the Chicago basis of rates and provide the most direct route to and from eastern centers. Cheap water transportation on the Great Lakes rounds out an ideal transportation system for Milwaukee. One-third of the total receipts and shipments of freight of Milwaukee is attributed to lake commerce, and, because of Milwaukee's partial dependence on water transportation, it is imperative that the city provide adequate facilities for the accommodation of steamships and cargoes.

RAILROADS SERVING MILWAUKEE

("With equal facilities for handling, and with equal port charges, the port with the widest choice of transportation facilities to the interior will be the greatest port. It follows that there must be equal, universal and free movement between any pier and any railroad line. To this must be added universal connection with any warehouse, and free movement from one part to any other part.")

"Ports and Terminal Facilities,"
MAC ELWEE.

STEAM RAILROADS:

CHICAGO, MILWAUKEE, ST. PAUL & PACIFIC R. R. CO.
Milwaukee Railroad System—10,598.66 miles.
Capacity of Railroad yards and Terminals in Milwaukee—17,495 cars.
Lines electrically operated—660 miles over mountains on Pacific Coast Extension.
Pioneers in roller bearing passenger trains.

CHICAGO & NORTHWESTERN RAILWAY CO.
Northwestern Railroad System—10,214.43 miles.
Capacity of Railroad yards and Terminals in Milwaukee—3,500 cars.
Railroad serves central, middle and northwest.

MINNEAPOLIS, ST. PAUL & SAULT STE. MARIE RY. CO.
Soo System—4,347.95 miles.
The Soo Line operates its own trains, freight and passenger, with its own crews and equipment over the Milwaukee Road right-of-way from Rugby Junction, 27.6 miles from Milwaukee. By operating agreement with the Soo Line, the Milwaukee Road breaks up and makes up trains and switches cars to and from industries, connecting lines and team tracks. The Soo Line leases from the Milwaukee Road, warehouse number 2, located at West Water Street, for concentration of inbound and outbound freight.

CARFERRIES:

GRAND TRUNK MILWAUKEE CAR FERRY CO.
Grand Trunk Canadian National Railway System—22,683 miles.
Grand Trunk Railway System in the United States—1,195 miles.
Daily Car Ferry and Passenger service to and from Grand Haven, Michigan.
Fast freight service to and from eastern points, via Niagara Frontier.
Four car ferries in fleet. Capacity of each ferry—28 cars.
Two private car ferry slips at Milwaukee.

Capacity Milwaukee Terminal—400 cars.
Direct rail connection:
    Chicago & Northwestern R. R. Co.
    Chicago, Milwaukee, St. Paul & Pacific R. R. Co.
    Minneapolis, St. Paul & Sault Ste. Marie R. R. Co.
      (via Milwaukee R. R.—see Soo Line.)

PERE MARQUETTE CAR FERRY CO.

Pere Marquette Railway Company—2,243.64 miles.
Daily Car Ferry and Passenger service to and from Ludington, Mich.
Fast freight service to and from eastern points via Niagara Frontier.
Seven car ferries in fleet. Capacity of each ferry—28 cars.
One private car ferry slip at Milwaukee.
Capacity Milwaukee Terminal—120 cars.
Direct rail connection:
    Chicago, Milwaukee. St. Paul & Pacific Ry. Co.
    Minneapolis, St. Paul & Sault Ste. Marie Ry. Co.
      (via Milwaukee R. R.—see Soo Line.)
The two public car ferry slips on the outer harbor, now under construction, will provide the Pere Marquette Car Ferry Company with a direct connection with the Chicago & Northwestern Railway Company.

ELECTRIC RAILROADS:

THE MILWAUKEE ELECTRIC RAILWAY & LIGHT CO.

Fast and frequent passenger and merchandise express service to Sheboygan, Watertown, East Troy, Burlington, Kenosha and intermediate points. The Wisconsin Motor Bus Line supplements the service from the above named electric terminals to Fond du Lac, Beaver Dam, Madison, Janesville, Beloit, Lake Geneva and Waukesha.

CHICAGO, NORTH SHORE & MILWAUKEE RAILROAD CO.

Passenger and merchandise express service to Lake Shore cities between Chicago and Milwaukee. Branch line from Lake Bluff, Illinois, to Libertyville, Illinois.

LOCAL RAILROAD RATES
In Cents Per Hundred Pounds

FROM	TO	| CLASSES									
		1	2	3	4	5	A	B	C	D	E
Kansas City, Missouri	Chicago	1.21½	1.03½	.76	.51	.41½	.48½	.41½	.33½	.28	24½
	Milwaukee	1.21½	1.03½	.76	.51	.41½	.48½	.41½	.33½	.28	.24½
	Duluth	1.42½	1.20	.88	.59	.47½	.56½	.47½	.38½	.33½	.29½
Omaha, Nebraska	Chicago	1.21½	1.03½	.76	.51	.41½	.48½	.41½	.33½	.28	.24½
	Milwaukee	1.21½	1.03½	.76	.51	.41½	.48½	.41½	.33½	.28	.24½
	Duluth	1.21½	1.03½	.76	.52½	.41½	.48½	.41½	.33½	.28	.24½
Sioux City, Iowa	Chicago	1.21½	1.03½	.76	.51	.41½	.48½	.41½	.33½	.28	.24½
	Milwaukee	1.21½	1.03½	.76	.51	.41½	.48½	.41½	.33½	.28	.24½
	Duluth	1.21½	1.03½	.76	.52½	.41½	.48½	.41½	.33½	.28	.24½
Des Moines, Iowa	Chicago	.91½	.73	.55	.41½	.32½	.36½	.30½	.26	.21	.18½
	Milwaukee	.91½	.73	.55	.41½	.32½	.36½	.30½	.26	.21	.18½
	Duluth	1.18½	.94	.74	.51	.39½	.47½	.39½	.32½	.28	.24½
St. Louis, Missouri	Chicago	.79	.67	.53	.39½	.27½	.31½	.25½	.22	.18	.16
	Milwaukee	.88½	.75	.59½	.44½	.31	.35½	.29	.25	.20	.17½
	Duluth	1.18½	1.00½	.81	.52	.39½	.52	.39½	.35	.30	.26½
Denver. Colorado	Chicago	2.73½	2.20½	1.67	1.29½	1.02	1.22	.96	.82	.71½	.61
	Milwaukee	2.73½	2.20½	1.67	1.29½	1.02	1.22	.96	.82	.71½	.61
	Duluth	2.73½	2.20½	1.67	1.29½	1.02	1.22	.96	.82	.71½	.61

MILWAU

IARBOR

GRAIN RECEIVING AND SHIPPING

Milwaukee is one of the seven largest primary grain markets of the country. The territory tributary to Milwaukee is one of the most important grain producing territories in the world and it includes the most important surplus producing grain states of the United States. Milwaukee lies on the outer rim of this vast producing area and is favorably located, with excellent rail and water facilities for the movement of grain to the consuming and export centers.

Three chief factors in the development of a primary grain market are: Proximity to the producing area, rail and water transportation facilities and favorable rates, and a consumption demand. The producing territory from which most of the grain marketed at Milwaukee is shipped, includes Wisconsin, Minnesota, Iowa and South Dakota. Grain from this territory, and, as circumstances permit, from other sections, reach this market over the rails of three great railway systems, namely: The Chicago, Milwaukee, St. Paul and Pacific, the Chicago and Northwestern, and the Minneapolis, St. Paul and Sault Ste. Marie. In addition to the above railroads serving the producing area, these railroads have direct rail connections with all railroads in both the spring and winter wheat producing sections, with through rates, breaking at Milwaukee, from points of origin in those sections to the east and southeast, the direction of shipment of most of the grain handled by them and where the buying customers of the Milwaukee grain merchandisers are located.

Milwaukee is exceptionally well situated with respect to transportation facilities to the east, southeast and south, the general consuming territory of grain, having direct rail connections with railroads serving those territories. The additional advantages of waterborne transportation are reflected in the freight rates. The package freight rate to the eastern sections of the country is three to four cents per one hundred pounds less than the all-rail rate. The largest movement of grain from Milwaukee is by bulk freight water carriers to the eastern consuming and exporting centers. Movements of this character take a lower rate than the package freight rate or the movement by all-rail.

The Milwaukee Chamber of Commerce, which includes in its membership all the varied interests of the grain trade of the Milwaukee market, such as commission merchants, brokers, elevator operators, merchandisers, millers, malsters, etc., is one of the oldest business organizations of its kind in the middle west. It was first called the "Corn Exchange," and with this body as a nucleus, the Chamber of Commerce was organized in 1858. Milwaukee is a highly important corn market, and also a market for barley, associated with the fact that this is the leading malt manufacturing point in the country. There is an average of perhaps one cargo of foreign grown flax seed a year received by water. The shipments of grain by water from Milwaukee is an important factor in the activities of the Chamber of Commerce. The reconstruction and operation, late in 1926, of the Chicago, Milwaukee, St. Paul and Pacific grain elevator "E" has given grain shipments, by water to lower lake ports, considerable impetus.

SHIPSIDE GRAIN ELEVATORS
"KINNICKINNIC"

Owner .... Chicago & Northwestern Railway Co.
Operator .... Donahue-Stratton Co.
Location .... Kinnickinnic Basin.
Type of Construction.............. Concrete.
Depth of Water in Berth........... 21 feet.
Storage Capacity .... 1,250,000 bushels.
Equipment .... 6 Marine loading spouts.

Loading Capacity per hr. (Boats)....90,000 Bushels.
Railroad Connection ....Chicago & Northwestern Railway
Tracks at Elevator
          Number 6
          Car Capacity 120
Superintendent ....H. H. Hicks.

"RIALTO"

Owner ....Chicago & Northwestern Railway Co.
Operator ....Donahue-Stratton Co.
Location ....Milwaukee River.
Type of Construction..............Wood—Concrete.
Depth of Water in Berth............19 feet.
Storage Capacity ....1,500,000 Bushels.
Equipment ....4 Marine loading spouts.
Loading Capacity per hr. (Boats)....40,000 Bushels.
Railroad Connection ....Chicago & Northwestern Railway.
Tracks at Elevator
          Number 2
          Car Capacity 15
Superintendent ....H. H. Hicks

"ELEVATOR E"

Owner ....C. M. St. P. & P. Railway Co.
Operator ....Cargill Grain Co.
Location ....South Menomonee Canal.
Type of Construction..............Concrete.
Depth of Water in Berth............21 feet.
Storage Capacity ....1,500,000 Bushels.
Equipment ....4 Marine loading spouts.
Loading Capacity per hr. (Boats)....50,000 Bushels.
Railroad Connection ....C. M. St. P. & P. Railway Co.
Tracks at Elevator
          Number 5
          Car Capacity 200
Superintendent ....L. M. Cote.

Shipments of Grain by Carferry

	Total Bu.	Wheat Bu.	Corn Bu.	Oats Bu.	Barley Bu.	Rye Bu.
1918	7,511,194	180,897	1,072,247	5,164,809	952,417	140,824
1919	12,639,205	830,971	1,098,221	9,048,400	1,475,403	186,210
1920	8,241,697	519,504	1,773,853	4,995,787	415,268	537,285
1921	3,575,861	281,159	1,086,195	1,768,587	360,730	79,190
1922	4,271,437	299,025	904,539	2,522,605	480,275	64,993
1923	3,771,160	233,201	974,899	2,128,957	201,576	142,527
1924	3,651,284	245,627	798,032	2,153,646	420,702	33,277
1925	2,714,604	311,157	359,821	1,666,752	339,796	37,078
1926	2,158,226	411,724	160,776	1,334,349	160,741	90,636
1927	3,357,450	337,995	191,723	1,867,428	821,917	138,387

Break-Bulk Shipments of Grain
(Pere Marquette Across-Lake)

	Total Bu.	Wheat Bu.	Corn Bu.	Oats Bu.	Barley Bu.	Rye Bu.
1918	217,125	......	......	217,125	......	......
1919	180,750	......	......	180,750	......	......
1920	74,000	......	......	74,000	......	......
1921	253,556	......	150,006	70,050	......	33,500
1922	1,852,933	..:....	1,117,444	433,675	257,814	44,000
1923	932,860	......	427,806	378,875	......	126,179
1924	1,314,545	169,356	238,821	622,668	263,700	20,000
1925	418,675	53,903	61,464	220,975	82,333	......
1926	352,330	114,530	63,000	174,800	......	......
1927	264,162	67,162	20,000	85,000	52,000	40,000

Lake Grain Shipments

	Total Bu.	Wheat Bu.	Corn Bu.	Oats Bu.	Barley Bu.	Rye Bu.
1918	18,513,613	6,549,791	415,600	11,293,481	254,741	......
1919	6,847,092	1,673,631	449,934	2,796,259	1,413,136	514,132
1920	3,200,887	394,515	1,050,311	686,325	115,425	954,311
1921	30,997,769	6,747,491	16,908,712	5,485,624	680,904	1,175,038
1922	16,270,680	464,411	11,436,131	3,420,339	440,390	509,409
1923	7,219,400	101,054	3,685,441	3,202,800	130,105	100,000
1924	13,000,251	6,245,083	3,549,240	1,367,659	843,921	1,084,348
1925	7,537,014	1,325,840	960,319	4,185,491	391,135	674,229
1926	8,993,564	6,329,600	1,192,683	1,220,852	84,439	165,990
1927	16,251,731	5,922,923	3,163,738	5,625,254	634,377	905,439

RECAPITULATION

	Total Bu.	Carferry Bu.	Break-Bulk Bu.	Lake Bu.
1918	26,241,932	7,511,194	217,125	18,513,613
1919	19,667,047	12,639,205	180,750	6,847,092
1920	11,516,584	8,241,697	74,000	3,200,887
1921	34,827,186	3,575,861	253,556	30,997,769
1922	22,395,050	4,271,437	1,852,933	16,270,680
1923	11,923,420	3,771,160	932,860	7,219,400
1924	17,966,080	3,651,284	1,314,545	13,000,251
1925	10,670,293	2,714,604	418,675	7,537,014
1926	11,504,120	2,158,226	352,330	8,993,564
1927	19,873,343	3,357,450	264,162	16,251,731

COAL

Milwaukee is the largest coal receiving port on Lake Michigan, and the second largest receiving port on the Great Lakes. Normally, about 4,000,-000 tons of coal is received annually by lake vessels, of which about sixty-five per cent is consumed locally and the balance shipped by rail to adjacent territory.

The coal originates, primarily in the bituminous fields of the Appalachian trough and the anthracite fields of Pennsylvania. Considerable coal from these districts move to the Lake Erie Ports in solid trainloads, frequently of sixty-five to seventy-five cars per train. Prompt attention is afforded lake cargo coal in order to promote efficiency and co-ordination between cars and vessels, thus reducing car detention at the ports to a minimum. The loading of coal at lower lakes is done mechanically, by dumping machines which dump whole carloads of coal at a single operation. The coal unloading equipment at the upper lake ports has been brought to a high degree of efficiency. Approximately seventy-five per cent of the coal received in Milwaukee is bituminous which arrives in bulk carriers from the principal Lake Erie ports; the balance of twenty-five per cent, anthracite, arrives in like manner but from Buffalo, N. Y., which port is the principal anthracite shipping port, due to its proximity to the anthracite region and its accessibility by the large bulk freight carriers.

Lake freight rates on coal are notably low because of the unbalanced trade of the lakes and the competition among carriers for westbound cargoes. Among the reasons for low cost of bulk freight transportation on the lakes are: First, the development of large standardized vessels of economical construction, having unusually large proportion of cargo space, and operated economically with relatively small crews; second, the development of economical and rapidly operated freight handling facilities at ports, such that the stay in port of vessels is reduced to a minimum. The lake freight rate on coal from Lake Erie to Lake Michigan ports is higher than to Lake Superior ports, due to the inability of vessels to secure sufficient return bulk cargo at Lake Michigan Ports.

Coal is also received at Milwaukee via carferry and all-rail, thus giving Milwaukee a continued assurance of having sufficient coal at all times. Diversified transportation routes are essential to industrial stability and community progress. The stocks of the local coal dock operators are often replenished in case of urgent need by resorting to the quicker service of carferry and all-rail.

MILWAUKEE COAL RECEIPTS
In short tons

	CARFERRY		ALL RAIL		LAKE		
Year	Anthracite	Bituminous	Anthracite	Bituminous	Anthracite	Bituminous	Total
1914	7,669	150,995	13,328	237,524	1,061,704	3,888,874	5,360,094
1915	57,271	154,912	3,532	189,625	1,088,434	3,776,771	5,270,545
1916	97,256	262,568	4,847	241,327	853,217	3,737,167	5,196,382
1917	64,047	174,144	2,621	984,992	922,538	3,025,558	5,173,900
1918	61,109	113,054	1,245	727,606	839,092	3,446,061	5,188,166
1919	91,264	218,086	2,228	530,708	985,692	3,174,078	5,002,056
1920	90,174	315,632	5,058	1,049,906	873,003	2,375,978	4,709,751
1921	141,736	253,778	3,244	794,934	1,023,645	2,574,374	4,791,411
1922	108,620	272,664	879	428,805	360,070	2,331,407	3,502,445
1923	249,738	575,655	7,541	789,569	966,224	3,238,722	5,827,449
1924	245,966	465,219	21,703	509,628	821,962	2,596,432	4,660,910
1925	247,506	487,001	51,579	488,272	490,534	3,196,767	4,959,669
1926	141,334	633,401	74,686	485,553	821,982	3,211,826	5,368,782
1927	43,824	449,207	80,207	687,007	502,209	4,249,133	6,011,587

MENOMONEE RIVER

COAL DOCKS

Milwaukee-Western Fuel Co.—Wells Bldg. .

1—Cherry Street Dock.

    Location—No. 1 Cherry Street, Milwaukee River.
    Dock Frontage: 635 feet.
    Depth of water at dock—19 feet, 6 inches.
    Unloading equipment—6 Portable Johnson Towers, 6 one ton clam
      shells.
    Unloading capacity per 10 hours—5.000 tons.
    Storage capacity—Anthracite—30,000 tons; Bituminous—45,000
      tons.
    Superintendent—W. F. Ardern.

2—Washington Street Dock.

    Location—Foot of Washington Street, Kinnickinnic River.
    Dock Frontage—500 feet.
    Depth of water at dock—19 feet, 6 inches.
    Unloading equipment—Mead-Morrison Mfg. Co. electric portable
      towers.; One 5 ton and two 2 ton clam shells.
    Unloading capacity per 10 hours—5,000 tons.
    Storage capacity—Bituminous—250,000 tons.
    Box car loaders—One Ottumwa and one Manierre.
    Locomotive crane—One 1 ton Brown Hoist.
    R. R. Connection—C. & N. W.
    Superintendent—W. F. Ardern.

3—Kinnickinnic Avenue Dock.

    Location—812 Kinnickinnic Ave., Kinnickinnic River.
    Dock frontage—548 feet.
    Depth of water at dock—19 feet.
    Unloading equipment—5 Portable Steel Johnson towers; 5 One
      ton clam shells.
    Unloading capacity per 10 hours—5,000 tons.
    Storage capacity—Anthracite—40,000 tons; Bituminous—35,000
      tons.
    Box car loaders—One John Ecks.
    R. R. Connection—C. & N. W.
    Superintendent—W. F. Ardern.

4—Commerce Street Dock.

    Location—772 Commerce St. Holton St. Bridge.
    Dock frontage—1.200 feet.
    Depth of water at dock—19 feet.
    Unloading equipment—Hyle & Patterson, Inc.: Electrical portable
      bridges; 2 one and one-half ton clam shells.
    Unloading capacity per 10 hours—2,000 tons.
    Storage capacity—Bituminous—65,000 tons.
    R. R. Connection—C. M. St. P. & P.
    Superintendent—W. F. Ardern.

5—Greenfield Avenue Dock.

    Location—Foot of Greenfield Avenue.
    Dock frontage—1.200 feet.
    Depth of water at dock—19 feet, 6 inches.
    Unloading equipment—Hyle & Patterson, Inc.; 3 two ton portable
      bridges.
    Unloading capacity per 10 hours—3,500 tons.
    Storage capacity—Bituminous—150,000 tons.
    Box car loaders—One Mannierre.

Locomotive crane—One 1 ton Brown Hoist
R. R. Connection—C. & N. W.
Superintendent—W. F. Ardern.

6—13th Street Dock.
    Location—Foot of 13th Street, Muskego Avenue Bridge.
    Dock frontage—1,200 feet.
    Depth of water at dock—19 feet, 6 inches.
    Unloading equipment—Mead-Morrison Mfg. Co. 1 ten ton clam
        shell.
    Unloading capacity per 10 hours—5,000 tons.
    Storage capacity—Bituminous—200,000 tons.
    R. R. Connection—C. M. St. P. & P.
    Superintendent—W. F. Ardern.

7—16th Street Anthracite Dock.
    Location—20th Street at Mt. Vernon.
    Dock frontage—1,250 feet.
    Depth of water at dock—19 feet, 6 inches.
    Unloading equipment—Mead-Morrison Mfg. Co., 2 two ton clam
        shells.
    Unloading capacity per 10 hours—6,000 tons.
    Storage capacity—Anthracite—90,000 tons.
    Box car loaders—One Manierre.
    R. R. Connection—C. M. St. P. & P.
    Superintendent—W. F. Ardern.

8—16th Street Bituminous Dock.
    Location—Foot of 16th Street at 16th St. Viaduct.
    Dock frontage—1,250 feet.
    Depth of water at dock—19 feet, 6 inches.
    Unloading equipment—One Hyle & Patterson, Inc., One Mead-
        Morrison Mfg. Co., One six ton Portable Tower, One eight ton
        Portable Tower.
    Unloading capacity per 10 hours—6,000 tons.
    Storage capacity—Bituminous—150,000 tons.
    Box car loaders—One Ottumwa and One Christie.
    R. R. Connection—C. M. St. P. & P.
    Superintendent—W. F. Ardern.

Lehigh Valley Coal Sales Co., 425 East Water Street.
Canal Street Dock.
    Location—South Menomonee River.
    Dock frontage—750 feet.
    Depth of water at dock—19 feet.
    Unloading equipment—Two Mead-Morrison Hoists; two ton clam
        shells.
    Unloading capacity per 10 hours—5,000 tons.
    Storage capacity—Anthracite—75,000 tons; Bituminous 5,000 tons.
    R. R. Connection—C. M. St. P. & P., C. & N. W. and Sault Ste.
        Marie.
    Superintendent—C. O. Hanson.

Philadelphia & Reading Coal & Iron Co., Majestic Bldg.
    Location of dock—West 16th Street Viaduct, North Menomonee
        River.
    Dock frontage—985 feet.
    Depth of water at dock—20 feet.
    Unloading equipment—Four Brown Hoists, 2 ton clam shells.
    Unloading capacity per 10 hours—3,000 tons.
    Storage capacity—Anthracite—75,000 tons.

Wis. Great Lakes Coal & Dock Co., Empire Bldg.

    Location of dock—Canal St. at 20th St.
    Dock frontage—2,500 feet.
    Depth of water at dock—20 feet.
    Unloading equipment—2 Mead-Morrison bridges, 10 ton clam shells.
    Unloading capacity per 10 hours—10,000 tons.
    Storage capacity—335,000 tons.
    R. R. Connection—C. M. St. P. & P., C. & N. W. and Sault Ste.
      Marie.
    Superintendent—Geo. A. Duval.

Callaway Fuel Co., 675 East Water Street.

    Location of dock—Cherry Street Bridge.
    Dock frontage—517 feet.
    Depth of water at dock—19 feet.
    Unloading equipment—One electric bridge, Lakeside Bridge and
      Steel, 3½ ton clam shells.
    Unloading capacity per 10 hours, 2,500 tons.
    Storage capacity, soft coal, 20,000 tons.
    Storage capacity, hard coal, 15,000 tons.
    Superintendent—Al. Schroeder.

Youghiogheny & Ohio Coal Co., 617 Colby-Abbot Bldg.

    Location of dock—South Menomonee River.
    Dock frontage—735 feet.
    Depth of water at dock—21 feet.
    Unloading equipment—Two Mead-Morrison Bridges, 5 ton clam
      shells.
    Unloading capacity per 10 hours—6,000 tons.
    Storage capacity—150,000 tons.
    R. R. Connection—C. M. St. P. & P., C. & N. W. and Sault Ste.
      Marie.
    Superintendent—Anthony Jaeck.

United Coal & Dock Co., No. 8 Wells Street.

  1—Gross Dock.
    Location—Menomonee River—6th Street Bridge.
    Dock frontage—430 feet.
    Depth of water at dock—20 feet.
    Unloading equipment—Four Mead-Morrison Portable Towers—1½
      ton clam shells.
    Unloading capacity per 10 hours—Bituminous 3,000 tons; Anthra-
      cite—5,000 tons.
    Storage capacity 150,000 tons.
    R. R. Connection—C. M. St. P. & P., C. & N. W. and Sault Ste.
      Marie.
    Superintendent—Dick Bosch.

  2—Independent Dock.
    Location—Kinnickinnic River, National Ave.
    Dock frontage—765 feet.
    Depth of water at dock—21 feet.
    Unloading equipment—2 Electric Bridges, Lakeside Bridge &
      Steel, 3½ ton clam shells.
    Unloading capacity per 10 hours—5,000 tons.
    Storage capacity—250,000 tons.

R. R. Connection—C. & N. W., C. M. St. P. & P., and Sault Ste. Marie.

Superintendent—J. Bosch.

3—West Side Dock.
  Location—West Menomonee River, 25th Street.
  Dock frontage—600 feet.
  Depth of water at dock—20 feet.
  Unloading equipment—Three Brown Hoists, two ton clam shells, 1 ton buckets.
  Unloading capacity per 10 hours—5,000 tons.
  Storage capacity—300,000 tons.
  R. R. Connection—C. M. St. P. & P., C. & N. W., and Sault Ste. Marie.
  Superintendent—J. J. Botsch.

Fellenz Coal & Dock Co., 1256 Bremen Street.
  Location of dock—Milwaukee River, Racine St. Bridge.
  Dock frontage—307 feet.
  Depth of water at dock—20 feet.
  Unloading equipment—1 Lakeside Bridge and Steel Electric Tower, 3¼ ton clam shells.
  Unloading capacity per 10 hours—4,000 tons.
  Storage capacity—52,000 tons.
  R. R. Connection—C. M. St. P. & P.
  Superintendent—L. Rauscher.

Schlitz Beverage Co., 215 Galena Street.
  Location of dock—Milwaukee River.
  Dock frontage—565 feet.
  Depth of water at dock—19 feet.
  Unloading equipment—One Portable Bridge Type, one ton clam shells.
  Unloading capacity per 10 hours—1,200 tons.
  Storage capacity—65,000 tons.
  R. R. Connection—C. M. St. P. & P.
  Superintendent—W. B. Uihlein.

Milwaukee Coke & Gas Co., 187 Greenfield Avenue.
  Location of dock—Greenfield Ave., Kinnickinnic River.
  Depth of water at dock—19 feet.
  Unloading equipment—Two Brown Hoists, One Johnson Electric Tower, 3½ ton clam shells.
  Unloading capacity per 10 hours—5,000 tons.
  Storage capacity—450,000 tons.
  R. R. Connection—C. & N. W., C. M. St. P. & P., and Sault Ste. Marie.
  Superintendent—E F. Burdick

PACKAGE FREIGHT

Under the Panama Canal Act of 1912, railroads were obliged to relinquish control of their Great Lakes steamship lines, which separation was accomplished by 1916. The immediate effect of this dissociation was the transfer of a considerable amount of freight, hitherto moving by lake and rail routes, to all-rail routes, thus causing a substantial reduction in the volume of package freight business on the lakes. The struggle of the private steamship lines to secure cargo is reflected in the increased growth of package freight receipts and shipments at Milwaukee. In recent years, a law became effective, compelling the railroads to make through lake and rail rates and to issue bills of lading to shippers using independent lines of steamers. The result of that law provided a better working arrangement between the steamship companies in securing a more equitable distribution of the through rates, thus enabling them to increase their tonnage. In 1927, Milwaukee ranked first among the port cities on the Great Lakes in receipts and shipments of package freight. The natural advantage of the cheap lake transportation of package freight is again manifest, and, with improved dock facilities and handling equipment, this service will become increasingly of more economic importance.

PACKAGE FREIGHT
By Water.

	RECEIPTS (short tons)	SHIPMENTS (short tons)	TOTAL (short tons)
1918	75,081	51,468	126,349
1919	98,504	55,513	154,017
1920	147,552	104,210	251,762
1921	158,749	151,103	309,852
1922	193,196	345,307	538,503
1923	221,391	368,990	590,381
1924	230,819	367,998	598,817
1925	286,044	361,187	647,231
1926	272,072	411,204	683,276
1927	307,999	472,768	780,767

STEAMSHIP COMPANIES

Canada Atlantic Transit Company,
5 West Water Street,
Tel. Broadway 7610.

Operating four steamships in service from Milwaukee to Depot Harbor, Ontario, carrying package freight on a schedule of three to four sailings per week during the season of navigation.

Goodrich Transit Company,
Foot of Michigan Street,
Tel. Broadway 7584.

A passenger and package freight service operating all the year round from Milwaukee to Racine and Chicago. During the summer season, June 25th to Labor Day, seventeen sailings per week; during the winter season, six sailings per week.

Great Lakes Transit Corporation,
19 West Water Street,
Tel. Broadway 7447.

A package freight line between Milwaukee and Erie, Pennsylvania and Buffalo, New York. Nine steamships in service, averaging five weekly sailings during the season of navigation.

Nicholson Universal Steamship Company,
225 Erie Street,
Tel. Broadway 6290.

Regular steamship service carrying automobiles and package freight between Milwaukee and Detroit, Michigan, and Toledo, Ohio. Operating eleven steamships with four regular weekly sailings during the season of navigation.

Pere Marquette Line Steamers,
68 West Water Street,
Tel. Broadway 7720.

A passenger and package freight line operating from Milwaukee to Ludington and Manistee, Michigan; two steamships in fleet. Maintains three sailings per week during the summer season and one a week in winter.

West Ports Steamship Line,
54 West Water Street,
Tel. Broadway 7575.

Regular service between Milwaukee and Sturgeon Bay, Kenosha, Sheboygan, Manitowoc, Kewaunee and Chicago. Three steamships in fleet, averaging six weekly sailings north and six weekly sailings south during the year.

Wisconsin & Michigan Transportation Company,
54 West Water Street,
Tel. Broadway 7575.

Regular passenger and package freight service between Milwaukee and Muskegon and Grand Haven, Michigan. Two steamships in fleet averaging seven weekly sailings during the summer and three weekly sailings during the winter.

Terminals & Transportation Corporation of America,
144 Broadway,
Tel. Broadway 3498.

Automobile transportation from Detroit, Michigan, to Milwaukee. Operates a fleet of steamships during season of navigation.

DOCK WAREHOUSES

1. **Goodrich Transit Co.**

    Location—Foot of Michigan Street.
    Area—25,365 square feet dry storage.
    Dock frontage—425 feet on Milwaukee River.
    Depth alongside dock—20 feet.

2. **Pere Marquette Line Steamers.**

    Location—68 West Water Street.
    Area—20,540 square feet dry storage.
    Dock frontage—186 feet on Milwaukee River.
    Depth alongside dock—20 feet.

3. **Hanson Storage Co.**

    Location—Milwaukee River at Erie Street.
    Area—11,000 square feet dry storage.
    Dock frontage—840 feet on Milwaukee River.
    Depth alongside dock—20 feet.
    House served by C. & N. W. R. R. Co. trackage.
    Capacity of trackage—19 cars.
    Use—Nicholson-Universal S. S. Co.

4. **Terminal Warehouse Company.**

    Location—South Water and Clinton Streets.
    Area—1,600,000 cubic feet cold and dry storage.
    Dock frontage—300 feet on Milwaukee River.
    Depth alongside dock—20 feet.
    House served by Milwaukee Road trackage.
    Capacity of trackage—10 cars.

5. **Chicago & Northwestern Dock Warehouse.**

    Location—Milwaukee River at South Water Street.
    Area—81,600 square feet dry storage.
    Dock frontage—600 feet on Milwaukee River.
    Depth alongside dock—20 feet.
    Capacity of trackage—35 cars.
    Interchange or transfer of freight with all boat lines.

6. **Chicago, Milwaukee, St. Paul & Pacific Dock Warehouses.**
    House No. 3 (North)

    Location—West Water Street at Milwaukee River.
    Area—42,940 square feet dry storage.
    Dock frontage—250 feet on Milwaukee River.
    Depth alongside dock—20 feet.
    Occupant—West Ports Steamship Line, Wisconsin-Michigan Transportation Co.

    House No. 4.

    Location—Menomonee River at West Water Street.
    Area—26,389 square feet dry storage.
    Dock frontage—400 feet on Menominee River.
    Depth alongside dock—20 feet.
    House served by the Milwaukee Road trackage.
    Capacity of trackage—6 cars.
    Occupant—Canada Atlantic Transit Co.

House No. 5.

Location—Menomonee River.
Area—22,725 square feet dry storage.
Dock frontage—450 feet on Menominee River.
Depth alongside dock—20 feet.
House served by the Milwaukee Road trackage.
Capacity of trackage—Dock houses 5 and 10—69 cars.
Leased to no specific water carrier but reserved for in-freight
from steamships during season of navigation.
Used for storage by railway company during winter months.

House No. 8.

Location—Menomonee Canal and Reed Street Yard.
Dock frontage—450 feet on Menomonee River.
Area—24,855 square feet dry storage.
Dock frontage—363 feet on Menomonee Canal.
Depth alongside dock—20 feet.
House served by Milwaukee Road trackage.
Capacity of trackage—Houses 8 and 9—28 cars.
Use—Milwaukee Road to deliver out-freight to the Great Lakes
Transit Corporation during season of navigation. Used for
storage during winter months.

House No. 9.

Location—Menomonee Canal at Reed Street Yard.
Area—11,985 square feet dry storage.
Dock frontage—233 feet on Menomonee Canal.
Depth alongside dock—20 feet.
House served by Milwaukee Road trackage.
Capacity of trackage—Houses 8 and 9—28 cars.
Use—Same as house No. 8.

House No. 10.

Location—Menomonee River at Sixth Street.
Area—35,750 square feet dry storage.
Dock frontage—608 feet on Menomonee River.
Depth alongside dock—20 feet.
House served by Milwaukee Road trackage.
Capacity of trackage—Houses 5 and 10—69 cars.
Occupant—Great Lakes Transit Corporation.

House No. 14.

Location—South Menomonee Canal and Reed Street Yard.
Area—19,635 square feet dry storage.
Dock frontage—255 feet on South Menomonee Canal.
Depth alongside dock—20 feet.
House served by Milwaukee Road trackage.
Capacity of trackage—8 cars.
Use—Milwaukee Road to deliver out-freight for the Canada At-
lantic Transit Company during season of navigation. Used
for storage during closed season.

House No. 15.

Location—8th Street and Menomonee Canal.
Area—11,312 square feet dry storage.
Dock frontage—202 feet on Kneeland Canal.
Depth alongside dock—20 feet.
House served by Milwaukee Road trackage.
Capacity of trackage—29 cars.
Use—Milwaukee road for storage throughout the year.

SHIP YARD AND REPAIR FACILITIES

MILWAUKEE DRY DOCK COMPANY
   (Subsidiary of the American Ship Building Company.)
   Superintendent—John Sinclair.
   Location—Foot of Washington Street, Kinnickinnic Basin.

REPAIR FACILITIES:
   Facilities for making repairs of all kinds to both wood and steel hulls
      and also machinery.

DRY DOCK: (Graving)
   Length over all—445 feet, 6 inches.
   Length of blocks—430 feet.
   Width of entrance at top—61 feet.
   Width of entrance at bottom—57 feet.
   Width of dock at top—85 feet.
   Depth over sill—14 feet, 6 inches.

LIMITING CONDITIONS:
   No limiting conditions for a vessel's entry to plant.

TUG BOAT SERVICE

Because of the narrow and winding rivers spanned by bascule, swing and railroad bridges, it is necessary for the larger vessels to employ the services of tug boats from the entrance of the rivers to berths and vice versa. The two tug boat companies provide twenty-four hour service during the season of navigation. Rates for tug boat hire may be had upon direct application to:

> Milwaukee Tug Boat Line,
> 98 Ferry Street,
> Tel. Broadway 1406.

> Edward E. Gillen Towing Company,
> 288 East Water Street,
> Tel. Broadway 4492.

STEVEDORING

The two local private stevedoring companies contract with lake carriers to load cargo from dock to vessel or discharge cargo from vessel to dock whenever such service is required by the carriers. Generally, the point of interchange between the lake and rail carriers is on the floor of the dock warehouse, and the cargo then requires handling into vessels or cars.

STEVEDORING COMPANIES:
   D. J. Nugent, foot of 6th St., Tel. Grand 554.
   S. H. DuPuy, 163 Davidson St., Tel. Broadway 2485.

WINTER MOORING OF VESSELS

The Milwaukee, Kinnickinnic and Menomonee Rivers are lined with docks which, after the close of navigation, are utilized for winter mooring of vessels. The charges for winter mooring may be had upon application to the various private dock property owners.

The Kinnickinnic Basin, which is part of the outer harbor project and under the jurisdiction of the Board of Harbor Commissioners, makes a desirable location for the mooring of vessels after the closing of navigation.

WINTER MOORING CHARGES
Kinnickinnic Basin
(From close to opening of navigation)

1—Berth alongside dock—30 cents per linear foot. Minimum charge—$125.00.

2—Berth alongside dock—Outside such vessel (1): 20 cents per linear foot. Minimum charge—$85.00.

3—Berth alongside dock—Outside such vessel (2): 15 cents per linear foot. Minimum charge—$60.00.

MAITLAND AIRPORT

The southern portion of the filled in harbor property of the north harbor tract is being used temporarily as Maitland Airport. The city of Milwaukee will eventually build a much larger and permanent airport in close proximity to the center of the city. Because of its limited area, the airport is being used as an emergency landing field for commercial, air mail, and passenger planes.

Maitland Airport is equipped with hangars, gasoline station, field house, border lights, flood lights, obstruction lights, beacon light, and a timber ramp for hydroplanes; three field attendants provide twenty-four hour service.

The field is in good landing condition; the surface is hard and has been carefully graded and rolled. The north and south runway is twenty-five hundred feet, and the east and west runway is nine-hundred feet.

No charges are made to planes for the use of the field. Maitland Airport is under the control and supervision of the Board of Harbor Commissioners, City of Milwaukee.

UNITED STATES GOVERNMENT, MUNICIPAL, AND OTHER AGENCIES RELATING TO THE PORT OF MILWAUKEE

U. S. Government Agencies:

War Department:

Engineer's Office: Hdqrs. Milwaukee District-Federal Bldg.
District Engineer: Lieut. Col. J. J. Kingman, Tel. Broadway 8600.

Treasury Department:

Customs Division: Hdqrs. Wis. Customs District No. 37, Federal Bldg.
Collector of Customs: Walter J. Wilde, Tel. Broadway 8600.
Coast Guard: McKinley Park.
Captain William Kincaid, Tel. Lakeside 3807.
Public Health Service: Federal Building.
Dr. Robert J. Bach, Tel. Broadway 2223.
Internal Revenue: District of Wisconsin, Federal Building.
Collector: A. H. Wilkinson, Tel. Broadway 4965.

Department of Commerce:

Bureau of Lighthouses: Hdqrs. 12th District, Federal Bldg.
Superintendent: Captain C. S. Hubbard, Tel. Broadway 8600.
Steamboat Inspection Service: Federal Bldg., Tel. Broadway 8600.
Inspectors:
Hulls—Captain F. W. Van Patten.
Boilers and Machinery—W. A. Collins.

Department of Agriculture:

Weather Bureau: Federal Building, Tel. Broadway 8600.
Meteorologist: Wm. P. Stewart.
Bureau of Agricultural Economics: 93 E. Michigan St.
Grain Supervisor: John T. Cavanagh. Tel. Broadway 1100.

Department of Justice:

District Judge: F. A. Geiger, Federal Bldg., Tel. Broadway 8600.
District Attorney: Levi H. Bancroft, Tel. Broadway 8600.
U. S. Marshall: R. J. White, Tel. Broadway 2670.

Municipal Agencies:

Board of Harbor Commissioners, City Hall, Tel. Broadway 3715.
President: Wm. Geo. Bruce, Tel. Broadway 3550.
Secretary: Ernest Bruncken.
Harbor Engineer: F. A. Kaiser.
Harbor Terminal Director: C. U. Smith.
Harbor Traffic Director: K. A. Albrecht.
Department of Public Works, City Hall, Tel. Broadway 3715.
Deputy Commissioner: David McKeith.
Harbor Master: Thomas Garrity, Tel. Broadway 1406.

Other Agencies:

Chamber of Commerce (Grain exchange) 93 Michigan Street.
Secretary: H. A. Plumb, Tel. Broadway 4446.
Transportation Department:
Manager: J. L. Bowlus, Tel. Broadway 4446.

Milwaukee Association of Commerce, 190 second St., Tel. Brdy. 5100.
Executive Director: Harry J. Bell.
Transportation Division—Manager: H. W. Gehrke.
Waterways Committee—Secretary: H. W. Gehrke.
Foreign Trade Division—Manager: B. P. Boykin.
Trade Promotion.
Co-operative Office-Bureau of Foreign & Domestic Commerce.

Milwaukee Harbor & Rivers Association, 120 E. Wis. Ave.
President: W. F. Ardern, Tel. Broadway 2850.
Secretary: Raymond H. Weins, Tel. Broadway 4492.

World Trade Club of Milwaukee.
President: Wm. Hinrichs, Tel. Orchard 8460.
Secretary: J. P. Torres, Tel. Kilbourn 5440.

Foreign Governments:
Consuls:
Mexico: E. P. Kirby Hale, 125 E. Wis. Ave., Tel. Brdy. 3970.
Italy: Angelo Cerminara, 445 Milwaukee St., Tel. Brdy. 2606.

Vice Consul:
Norway: Olaf I. Rove, Tel. Broadway 3320.

Honorary Vice Consul:
Brazil: Lewis Sherman, Tel. Broadway 4200.

Consular requirements: Call Consular Offices and where no local representative is to be had, call the Association of Commerce, Foreign Trade Division, Tel. Broadway 5100.

Customhouse Brokers:
Dey, M. E. & Co., 141 E. Wisconsin Ave., Tel. Broadway 8687.
Salentine & Salentine, 141 E. Wis. Ave., Tel. Broadway 2030.

Ship Masters Association: Lodge No. 6, 512 Mitchell Bldg.
Secretary: W. A. Ashley, 699 Cramer St., Tel. Lakeside 4746-R.

Marine Architects & Naval Engineers:
Pommer & Co., 221 Wisconsin Avenue, Grand 4243.

Steamship Agents:
Walter Fitzgerald, 373 Broadway, Tel. Broadway 512 or 134.
Vance & Joys, 373 Broadway, Tel. Broadway 3908.

Lake Carriers Association, 310 State Street, Tel. Grand 2360.
Commissioner: J. A. Berentsen, Res. Phone, Blmd. 186.

THE MILWAUKEE OUTER HARBOR PROJECT

HISTORICAL DEVELOPMENT OF THE MILWAUKEE
OUTER HARBOR

Because of the numerous disasters to shipping on Lake Michigan, Congress, in 1881, made provisions for the creation of a Harbor of Refuge in Milwaukee Bay by the extension of a breakwater across the Bay, from McKinley Beach at the north, in a southerly direction; succeeding acts of Congress provided additional appropriations for the completion of the breakwater project.

In 1900, Mayor David S. Rose recommended the construction of a system of docks and terminals in deep water outside of Jones Island because, as he stated, the rivers were growing inadequate to meet the demands of the increasing commerce. District Army Engineer, Colonel Warren, after making a study of the proposition, and in his report to the secretary of War, Elihu Root, declared against an outer harbor, which report was promptly approved by the Secretary of War. Mayor Rose persisted in the matter, however, and in the Spring of 1900 a committee of ten citizens was appointed to be known as the Permanent Harbor Improvement Committee; this Committee made a study of the project and after several months reported to the Mayor and the Common Council, recommending that the channels in the inner harbor be deepened, that the Federal Government be requested to make a permanent survey of Milwaukee harbor, and that permanent harbor lines be established. This Committee made no recommendation as to Jones Island and the outer harbor development. In August, 1903, Colonel Warren submitted a report to the Chief of the Engineers, outlining a number of improvements in the inner Harbor, among which were: The enlargement of the Kinnickinnic River to a width of two hundred feet; the construction thereon of two turning basins of sufficient size to accommodate six-hundred foot vessels; the widening of the Menominee River by the removal of a corner at the entrance of the South Menomonee Canal and the removal of another corner on the same channel just opposite the site of Milwaukee Road grain elevator "A." The city was required to acquire the lands necessary for widening the channels and creating turning basins after which the Government was to do the necessary dredging; this project was adopted by Congress March 3, 1905. The City of Milwaukee acquired several pieces of land necessary to the widening of the Kinnickinnic Basin, but aside from that, nothing was accomplished towards the realization of this project.

In May, 1908, the Common Council appointed a committee of five members to ascertain the cost of acquiring Jones Island and the feasibility of establishing harbor terminals thereon. At the same time a resolution was approved by the Common Council declaring in favor of an outer habor and directing the United States Government to make the preliminary survey looking to that end. Accordingly, Congress, in 1909, ordered another survey of the Milwaukee outer harbor project. In response to this authorization, the United States District Engineer, Major C. S. Bromwell, submitted a report on the preliminary survey, recommending that a plan and estimate of an outer harbor be prepared, inasmuch as, in his judgment, it was probable that such a harbor would be needed in the not far-distant future. In June, 1909, the Common Council, special committee of five, reported in favor of the acquisition of Jones Island and the establishment of municipal terminals thereon. The committe was promptly authorized to engage Isham Randolph, C. E., of Chicago, to make a full detailed engineering report and to submit a plan of development. This plan was submitted in the Spring of 1910, but the Common Council indefinitely postponed the resolution declaring in favor of an outer harbor, and rejected the Randolph plan.

In October, 1911, Mayor Emil Seidel, by previous authorization, appointed a Harbor Commission of nine citizens of Milwaukee, conversant with harbor and shipping matters, to study the needs of Milwaukee in regard to harbor facilities and to act in an advisory capacity to the Common Council. In Februry, 1912, the Harbor Commission was formally organized, and in the meantime the Common Council made financial provisions for the execution of its work. In May, 1912, this Harbor Commission rendered a report against the acquisition of Jones Island for outer harbor purposes, and recommended the development of the inner side of Jones Island, together with the deepening and revetting of Kinnickinnic Basin; also that immediate steps be taken to remedy certain conditions in the Menominee and Kinnickinnic Rivers. In making this report, the activities of the first Harbor Commission ceased, it having been declared an illegal body by the Common Council because the appointments to its membership were not confirmed by their Body.

On October 12, 1912, Mayor G. A. Bading, upon authorization by the Common Council, appointed a new harbor commission. This re-organized commission, after considerable study, urged the early acquirement of Jones Island by the city, because it offered the only remaining opportunity for the municipality to acquire water frontage capable of a comprehensive terminal development. Acting on this suggestion, the Common Council provided the necessary funds and ordered the condemnation of Jones Island as far south as the old harbor entrance. Before the proceedings started, the Sewerage Commission was given authority to acquire the north one-thousand feet of the Island for a municipal sewerage disposal plant. In August, 1914, this Commission effected an agreement between the Chicago & Northwestern Railroad and the City of Milwaukee, establishing a line showing the division of property of the north harbor tract. During its regime this Commission permitted the removal of obstructing corners on the Menomonee River and south Menomonee Canal, and served to establish a uniform system of harbor lines, construction of the rubblemound breakwater along the shore of Lake Michigan from Wisconsin Avenue to the harbor entrance; revetment of the inner side of Jones Island; bulk heading in the lake to protect the fill on the outside of Jones Island; a survey by the Federal Government to determine the need of additional breakwater protection at Milwaukee, condemnation of the north half of Jones Island and the inauguration of proceedings and condemnation of the lower half of the same as far south as Wilcox Street, and a legislative enactment granting authority to the City of Milwaukee to create a Board of Harbor Commissioners with power to plan harbor and waterway improvements and to provide for the construction of docks, wharves, warehouses, etc., subject to the approval of the Common Council. In June, 1919, this commission, by authorization of the Common Council, engaged Mr. H. Mc-Harding, of New York City, to study and prepare an engineering report and plans pertaining to the Milwaukee harbor project. The plans were received and submitted to the Common Council, and approved in June, 1920. This was the last act of this particular Harbor Commission.

The Board of Harbor Commissioners of the City of Milwaukee was created by the Common Council June 1, 1920, under authority granted by Chapter 289, Laws of Wisconsin, 1919. The membership of the Board is confined to five qualified electors of the City of Milwaukee with terms extending over a period of three years. Agreeable to the action of the Common Council, Mayor Daniel W. Hoan, on January 14, 1920, appointed five citizens to membership on the Board. In November, 1922, a contract was made for levelling the north harbor tract to an elevation of five feet above city datum. In June, 1923, Governor Blaine signed the bills which amended the Harbor Law and also Chapter 358 of the laws of Wisconsin—

1909, in which the State of Wisconsin cedes to the City, the title and interest of the State of Wisconsin to submerged lands extending into the lake for a distance of fifteen-hundred feet from the shore line for construction of harbor facilities. In 1924, a survey was conducted to determine the economic advantages and disadvantages of fixed bridges over the Milwaukee River north of Wisconsin Avenue. In January, 1924, a proposal was received by the Board of Harbor Commissioners from the Illinois Steel Company to exchange land owned by the City of Milwaukee for land owned by the Illinois Steel Company in lieu of condemnation. An agreement between the City and the Illinois Steel Company for the exchange of lands was entered into on March 15, 1926. The Illinois Steel Company property on Jones Island is the key property to developing rail connections. The Harbor Commission has been active in carrying out the essentials of this agreement. In the early part of 1926, the revetment on the inside of Jones Island was reinforced by two additional rows of anchorage. In November, 1927, the Abbott Tract, lying west and south of South Bay Street, was purchased by the City of Milwaukee for utilization by the Harbor Commission as a railroad interchange yard. In September, 1927, dredging and filling in of a certain area on Jones Island was undertaken under the supervision of this Commission, this being the first step in the development of carferry terminals on Jones Island.

BREAKWATER PROJECT

The original project for improvement of Milwaukee Harbor was adopted by the United States Government by act of March 3, 1843. The original project for the harbor of refuge was adopted by act of March 3, 1881. The existing breakwater project was authorized by the following river and harbor acts:

The act of August 30, 1852 provided for the north pier.

The act of March 3, 1881 provided for 7,600 feet of the north breakwater.

The act of March 3, 1889 provided for 19 foot channel dimensions.

The act of March 2, 1907 provided for the south pier and also provided for extending the north breakwater 1,000 feet.

The act of September 22, 1922 provided for extending and completing the north breakwater, for a south breakwater, and for deepening and widening the channel.

The river and harbor act of September 22, 1922, adopted the project for breakwater extension, construction and dredging, provided that actual work by the United States shall not be commenced thereon until the City of Milwaukee shall have presented evidence satisfactory to the Secretary of War, that it is prepared to finance and carry out its part of the project along the general lines of the plan presented to the 66th Congress, second session, subject, however, to such modifications as may be deemed essential by the Chief of Engineers, and that it will deed to the United States, the area proposed to be donated for federal uses just north of the north pier. These assurances have been given by the City of Milwaukee, and the city's plans were approved by the Assistant Secretary of War on April 5, 1923. .

The breakwater project provides for a north breakwater 10,370 feet long, and the construction of a south breakwater approximately 9,650 feet long, extending to the shore, thereby forming a protected basin in which is to be located a commercial harbor to be constructed by the City of Milwaukee. The width of entrance between the two breakwaters is 500 feet. It further provides for the protection of the river mouth by two piers which are 360 feet apart at their outer ends, and 575 feet apart at the shore line, about 1,656 feet and 1,608 feet in length for the north and south piers respectively, for a channel 21 feet deep, extending from that depth in the lake to the mouth of the river, a total length of about 2,850 feet, the width of the channel outside the piers to be 600 feet.

All work on the breakwater project has been completed with the exception of a portion of the extreme south end of the south breakwater, the south breakwater shore arm, and channel dredging and widening. It is anticipated that all construction work will be completed in the fall of 1929.

The breakwater is being constructed under the supervision of the local district engineer of the United States Army, and the approximate cost upon completion of the project is $5,000,000, which is borne by the United States Government.

53

OCEAN WATERWAY AND PORT OF MILWAUKEE

William George Bruce, President
Great Lakes Harbors Association.

The proposal to connect the Great Lakes with the Atlantic Ocean b
means of the Welland Canal and the St. Lawrence waterway is rapidl
approaching a stage of realization. The engineering problem connecte
therewith has been solved. The question of commercial utility has bee
established. The negotiations in progress between the United States an
Canada, have progressed to a point where a common appreciation as t
economic advantages which may accrue to the two countries has bee
reached.

In brief, two-thirds of the way toward an agreement has been travelle
The last lap now consists of the diplomatic preliminaries which will fin
expression in a treaty between the two countries, embodying the condition
relating to the construction and maintenance of the waterway and a
understanding as to the rights and equities involved.

The people of the United States have been made clear as to the advan
tage of affording the Midwest an outlet to the high seas. The St. Law
rance project will bring the Midwest one thousand miles nearer the sea
and thus afford a more direct and expeditious shipment of its product
to the markets of the world.

The economic advantage to be derived from a deep waterway projec
connecting the Great Lakes with the Atlantic Ocean is recognized by bot
countries, the United States and Canada. The late Presidents Woodro
Wilson and Warren G. Harding were enthusiastic in their support of th
St. Lawrence project. President Calvin Coolidge endorsed the project i
several of his public documents. The two great political parties warml
recognized the project in their national platforms. The opposition thus fa
manifested has been sectional rather than political. New York City op
poses the idea of developing the lake ports into ocean ports. This oppos
tion is based upon narrow and selfish lines and therefore cannot prevai
The St. Lawrence project is certain to become a magnificent reality.

The Dominion of Canada is committed to St. Lawrence deep waterwa
through the construction of the Welland Canal which when completed wi
cost that country something like one hundred and fourteen million dollar

But what about Milwaukee? In what way are we concerned in a projec
which will afford direct waterway communication between ourselves an
the ocean ports of the world? The answer is obvious. A great industri
center must have transportation connections with the outside world. I
products must be carried to the markets of the world economically an
expiditiously. An outlet to the sea will afford us closer connections wit
a coast-wise trade and more direct communication with the markets c
Europe.

But the port of Milwaukee is not only interested in securing a wider ou
let for its factory products; it is also concerned in finding a better mark
for Wisconsin's farm products, both at home and abroad. The prosperit
of the great state of Wisconsin means the prosperity of Milwaukee. Th
interests of agriculture and manufacture are reciprocal and mutual.

The city of Milwaukee and the state of Wisconsin figure to a conside
able degree in the total volume of the nation's import and export trad
Our products of both factory and farm now go to foreign lands. Our im
ports from other countries run into large figures. The commerce alread
established can be greatly increased and can be conducted more economi
ally if ocean ships can enter the harbor of Milwaukee directly and at t

same time enabling our own ships to carry our commodities directly to European ports, and to ocean coast-wise points.

When ships flying foreign flags are to arrive here we shall be ready to receive them. Not only will our harbor waters enjoy the requisite depth, but the port facilities will be sufficiently ample and complete to receive any cargo that may be brought here. No port on the Great Lakes will be better equipped to engage in a foreign trade than the port of Milwaukee.

OUTER HARBOR DEVELOPMENT

The new era in water transportation makes it imperative that Great Lakes Port Cities acquire their lake front properties as soon as practicable. The natural growth of the cities and the concurrent rise in land values may effectually retard cities from port development unless the property is immediately acquired with a view of utilization in the future. Simultaneous port development on the Great Lakes is highly desirable from the standpoint of promotion of waterborne commerce, and the efficiency of handling cargo and vessel tonnage, as between ports. It is, therefore, gratifying to note that many of the Great Lake Cities have comprehensive plans or are preparing plans for either private or public port development. Unless other port cities recognize this fact, they cannot hope to qualify for participation in the increasing commerce of the Great Lakes.

The City of Milwaukee has acquired its lake front property, and upon completion of revetting and filling in certain submerged portions, will have 231 acres of land with a frontage on Lake Michigan of 2½ miles, for the development of an outer commercial harbor. There are many reasons why the City of Milwaukee should develop its outer harbor property, namely:

Milwaukee has fewer railroads serving its industries and commercial houses than any other city of its size in the United States. The city is therefore partially dependent on water transportation to provide the necessary direct routes for distribution purposes. Over one-third of the total tonnage, receipts and shipments, is directly attributed to water transportation. Water transportation results in a tremendous annual saving in the city's freight bill.

The many openings and closings of bascule and swing bridges for the navigation of vessels on the Milwaukee, Kinnickinnic and Menomonee Rivers are becoming an obstacle to the continually increasing land traffic. Many delays are incurred by reason of the movement of vessels on the rivers, and it is to the interest of all Milwaukee, that wherever practicable, shipping be encouraged to utilize the outer harbor, thereby minimizing traffic on the rivers. In addition, the city is burdened with a large expense for maintenance of bridges, replacement of existing bridges, construction of new bridges, and the dredging and maintaining of a 21 foot channel depth.

There is a tendency toward increasing tonnage, and deeper draft vessels on the Great Lakes, which makes it exceedingly difficult for the larger vessels to navigate the narrow tortuous rivers of the Milwaukee inner harbor. As far as practicable, the tonnage should be encouraged to use the outer harbor, where deeper water and easier methods of operation are assured. Utilization of the outer harbor facilities will also reduce the turn-around of the vessels, which is an important factor in ship operation.

The waterborne commerce of the Port of Milwaukee has been showing a steady increase during the past few years, and, in order to provide for the natural increase in lake traffic, the outer harbor project will provide the necessary facilities and co-ordination between lake and rail transportation in order to accommodate the lake traffic.

The existing facilities on the inner harbor are becoming inadequate to accommodate the increasing lake traffic. New lake transportation lines are finding difficulty in locating suitable dock sites. Most of the dock facilities on the inner harbor are of a private character. A number of lake cities are developing more efficient facilities in handling lake traffic, and it is therefore important that Milwaukee develop comparable facilities in order to expedite the movement of cargo and vessels on the Great Lakes.

It is very important at this time that comprehensive plans be developed and facilities be planned for the time when the Great Lakes-St. Lawrence Ship Channel will become a reality. Ocean vessels will require a greater depth of water and easier methods of operation than is now provided in the channel of the existing inner harbor.

The City of Milwaukee has adopted a comprehensive outer harbor development plan, recommended by competent engineers. Adequate rail connections are fundamental in harbor development work, and the Board of Harbor Commissioners is striving to admit all railroads (now serving Milwaukee) to the outer harbor property on an equal basis, despite the many legal and physical obstacles. Direct access of all railroads to the outer harbor property will eliminate the existing interchange switching charge between the rail carriers, thus reducing the transportation costs and the time involved in making deliveries.

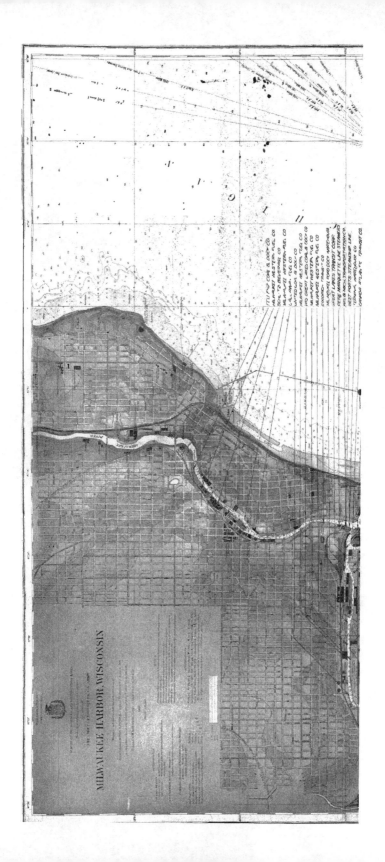

MILWAUKEE HARBOR, WISCONSIN

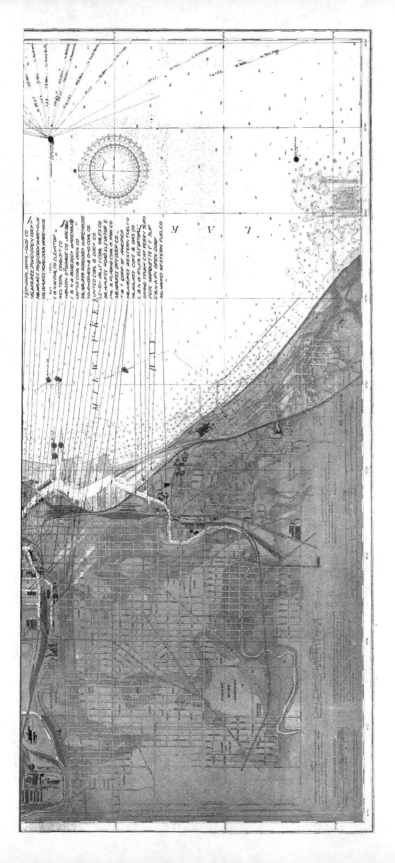

CPSIA information can be obtained
at www.ICGtesting.com
Printed in the USA
BVHW09s1956250718
522632BV00012B/154/P